London River

GAVIN WEIGHTMAN

London River

The Thames Story

C&B

COLLINS & BROWN

First published in Great Britain in 1990
by Collins & Brown Limited
Mercury House
195 Knightsbridge
London SW7 1RE

A CIP catalogue record for this book
is available from the British Library

ISBN 1 85585 075 3
First reprint 1990
Second reprint 1991
Editor Jennifer Chilvers

Picture Research Philippa Lewis

Art Director Roger Bristow

Designed by Sally Smallwood

Filmset by Tradespools, Frome
Reproduction by Fotographics, Hong Kong
Printed and bound in Italy by New Interlitho, Milan

CONTENTS

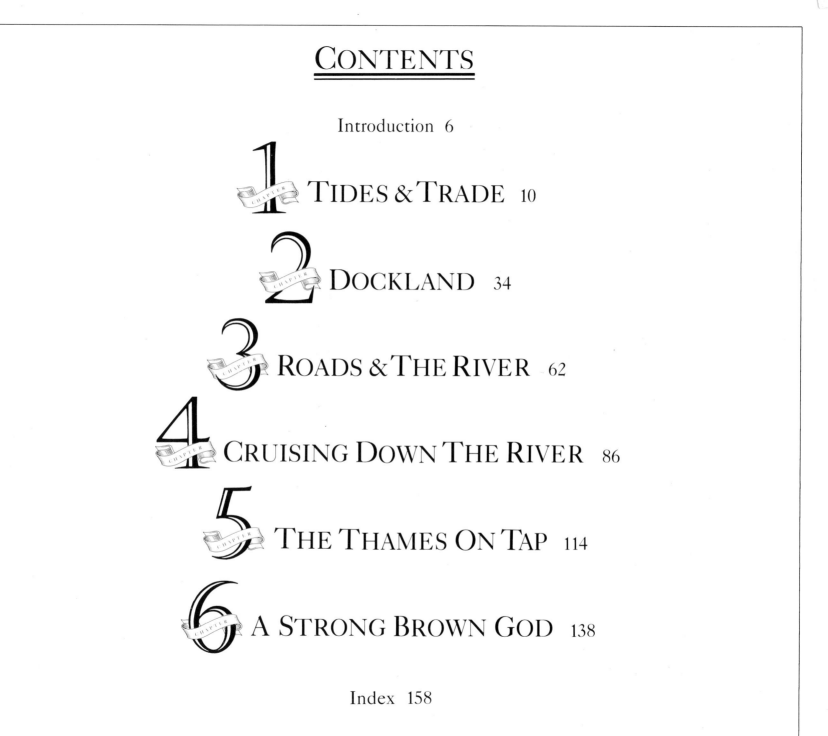

INTRODUCTION

Today there are few ships on the Thames to speak of: no liners nudging into the Pool of London, giants of the sea hauled on taut hawsers by little tugs. The few sailing barges carry tourists, no collier ships lower their funnels to clear London's bridges and London's docklands, which lay in ruins for a decade or more, have been reworked for offices, marinas and wind surfers. The warehousing has crumbled. The river is commercially dead, but ecologically alive again, home to fish, cormorants and duck.

Hardly anybody arrives in London by sea—in most people's minds the aeroplane replaced the ship, just as the railway replaced the river and the canal as a means of transport. That London appears to survive very well without its port gives the impression that ships and sailors are from our very distant past, and rivers and the sea have for England no serious use: now they are being redeveloped for fun.

Yet within recent memory London's port below Tower Bridge, not only the great expanse of dockland but the riverside north and south down to the Isle of Dogs and beyond to Tilbury, was the greatest in the world. Since the 1960s, international passenger and freight traffic have become sharply segregated, and we imagine everything goes by air these days. But a very high proportion of goods coming to Britain arrives by sea. That excludes the lorries which cross the Channel in the final stages of their journey from Europe. Airports ship people about; ships still handle most trade—oil, timber, cars, coal.

London's port has not entirely disappeared—much of it has simply gone out of sight, down the river to Tilbury, and the oil terminals and wharves of the estuary. There are far fewer ships because the tankers and liners are now gigantic and their goods are hidden away in great metal boxes: containers, weighing up to forty tons each.

Until the post-war years, the Thames was vital to London's expansion, and the whole of the navigable river from the sea to the upper reaches around Cricklade played a part in providing the city with food, water, building materials, luxury goods and valuable foreign trade. In the Middle Ages the great export was wool, and such legendary Londoners as Richard (Dick) Whittington—a mercer, several times Lord Mayor, and London benefactor—made money out of dealing in the export of woollen cloth.

As London grew, so did its port. Down-river from Old London Bridge, which straddled the Thames more like a barrier than a river

The Thames at Richmond in the early seventeenth century when the most luxurious form of travel was by river.

crossing, the ships that traded with other parts of Britain, with Europe and the East and West Indies, accumulated steadily until the river was crammed with masts often likened to a forest. Further downstream were the Woolwich Arsenal, the great ship-building yards of Blackwall and the naval dockyards of Chatham. Above London Bridge the Thames had a different kind of character with barges taking London's wealth inland and bringing back wood and cheese and malting barley.

London was never, however, just a port. It began as early as the late Middle Ages to develop a dominance in Britain quite unmatched by any major town in Europe. Everything accumulated in London, and its concentration of wealth influenced the development of farming and trade in the regions around it. This dominance had a great deal to do with the fact that it was on the Thames, and with the special nature of the river itself.

It is no coincidence that the royal palaces—Windsor, Hampton Court, Whitehall, Greenwich and others now long gone were built beside the Thames. The stone and timber for the building of Windsor Castle came up the river, and the royal barges, with their splendid

London became the greatest city in the world in the days of sailing ships. This was the scene in the Pool of London about 1840 when the first steamers had arrived. James Wilson Carmichael's painting shows a Thames barge, watermen carrying passengers, and the rigging of larger ocean-going ships.

decoration and liveried oarsmen, carried royalty and the luminaries of the court up and down the river in the days when roads were deeply rutted, unmetalled and often impassable in winter.

This early royal presence on the Thames was significant—it was truly a royal river—for it concentrated political power here. When this executive clout was combined with the trading wealth of the City, all influence and riches accumulated on the banks of the Thames.

By the Elizabethan era, London was a great city, with a world-famous bridge, and a great port. The influence of shipping and the sea pervaded everything, but the town was beginning to outgrow the port. When the docklands were built to the east of the City in the early nineteenth century, London had become a great metropolis supplied by a port which was a world apart. It was still absolutely vital to London's survival but it was segregated: in this period the East End was born, a region that moral crusaders of the Victorian era regarded as foreign as the countries from which much of its trade arrived. This was 'darkest England'.

In the eighteenth century watermen crowded the stairs down to the Thames crying 'oars' in their clamour for passengers to carry up and down the river, Hanoverian royalty were rowed in royal barges to the accompaniment of water music composed by Handel and the centre of London looked like Venice, its palaces with great terraces down to the river. By the mid-nineteenth century, all this had changed. The river had been bridged in many places, railways had captured the imagination of the age, and steamers had begun to destroy the watermen's trade.

THE RIVER DIVIDED AND BRIDGED

From the 1840s railways had undermined the commercial traffic of the Thames above Teddington, and it was rapidly becoming a playground for the Victorian middle classes. Books appeared extolling the great romantic pleasures of the 'sweet Thames', fishermen's punts became the vessels for Victorian leisure, anthropomorphic animals emerged along the banks with *The Wind in the Willows*, and the rowing regattas began. Socially, the Thames became divided: spice-scented, dangerous, horrifically exciting dockland, and lazy, serenaded, picnic strewn, twittering Henley.

In between, the Thames flowing through the centre of London was bridged out of existence: crossing the river became the obsession in the nineteenth century as the road traffic of the capital became jammed.

One of the last attempts to ease that problem, the construction of Tower Bridge in the 1890s, became by one of those odd quirks of historical fate, the symbol of London at the height of its dominance of the world. It is wonderfully evocative—anachronistically reflecting the architecture of the Norman Tower of London, a drawbridge for ships opening fifty times a day in its first year and crammed with horse-drawn carts crossing the river when the great steam-driven bascules were lowered.

It is a popular belief amongst Londoners that the Americans who, in the 1970s, bought the nineteenth-century London Bridge and shipped it out to Arizona brick by brick thought they were buying Tower Bridge. Though foreigners often confuse the famous Tower Bridge with Old London Bridge, the American syndicate that bought the nineteenth-century London Bridge knew what they were doing.

The story of the gullible Americans is one of the many myths about the river that continue to fascinate Londoners. They know the Thames was important, but they do not know why, so long have the lives of most of them been far removed from the ebb and flow of the tides, the rigging of ships or the working of oars. For one section of London, however, the life of the river which finally died in the 1960s lives on vividly in the memory. They sailed the ships, unloaded the sacks of sugar and boxes of tea, steered the lighters and as children played sandcastles by the river below Tower Bridge and even swam the treacherous water between Rotherhithe and Wapping. In this book, and the television series it accompanies, their memories bring the river alive in a way no other learning or analysis can.

But this is not simply another nostalgic journey down 'Old Father Thames'. Nor is it another tourist trip along the river with some famous landmarks pointed out along the way. It is about the manner in which the river has given rise to London, how it has itself changed over the centuries, and how today it continues to influence the life of the metropolis.

Historically the Thames may appear to be at its lowest ebb: redundant. But that is an illusion. As the industrial use of the river has dwindled, its wildlife has returned, it has become 'sweeter' again in the metropolitan reaches, and it will remain a massive resource and a potential power for both good and evil. A new era in the story of the river has begun, and the final chapter of this book is the first in the future history of the river.

The leisurely traffic jam at Henley Regatta in the 1890s. During the London Season, the upper reaches of the Thames were as crowded as the port.

In contrast to Henley, the industrial Thames from which London's wealth was created. Shipyard workers arriving at Blackwall in 1908.

TIDES & TRADE

It matters little today which way the wind blows through the mountainous steel and concrete blocks of the City of London's banks and financial institutions. Nor does the ebb and flow of the tides that swell the river and drag it back between the stone walls of the Embankment mean anything to the City's trade. Lloyd's, housed in its new building—lit up at night like an amusement park arcade—is still concerned about the fate of ships at sea, and traders in commodities still follow the fortunes of giant freighters carrying the goods on which they gamble. On the Baltic Exchange space on ships in all parts of the world is traded. The City hangs on to its association with the sea, but the ships no longer discharge their cargoes below London Bridge.

The great natural power of wind and tide troubles the City now only when gales rattle the glass windows of the tower blocks, or tidal flood waters rise unnervingly close to the river wall. Yet it was wind and tide that brought London's wealth, and continued to affect its fortunes right through the Victorian era when coal and steam had begun to transform the world and man-made power was making light of the force of the elements.

Of the many Victorian descriptions of the Thames, that of the extraordinary journalist Henry Mayhew, who surveyed London life in the 1850s, is one of the most evocative, if perhaps a bit flushed with the purple prose of the Victorians:

> *As I stood looking down upon the river the hundred clocks of the churches around me—with the golden figures on their black faces winking in the sunshine—chimed the hour of two in a hundred different tones, while solemnly, above all, boomed forth the monster bell of St Paul's, filling the air for minutes afterwards with a sweet melodious moan; and scarcely had it died away than there arose from the river the sharp tinkle of 'four bells' from the multitude of ships and steamers below. Indeed there was an exquisite charm in the different sounds that smote the ear from the busy Port of London. Now you would hear the tinkling of the distant purl-man's bell [a beer-seller on the river], as in his boat he flitted in and out among the several tiers of colliers. Then would come the rattle of some chain suddenly let go; after this, the chorus of many seamen heaving at the ropes, while, high above all, would be heard the hoarse voice of someone from the shore bawling through his hands to his mate aboard the craft*

The forest of masts of ships which brought wealth to the City of London. Thomas Luny's painting captures the crowded and bustling nature of the river just before the building of the docklands began.

in the river ... As you looked down on the endless vista of masts that crowded each side of the river you could not help feeling how every power known to man was used to buy and diffuse the riches of every part of the world over this little island.

Though the kind of shipping on the Thames had changed greatly by the earlier part of this century, there are still those who can recall leaving the port in a sailing vessel. At the age of nineteen, Robert Williamson left on the *Discovery*—a ship with both steam power and sails—from the West India Dock for Hudson Bay to bring back furs. That was in 1911.

I reported on board and the captain, John Ford, was there, a stocky, bearded gentleman, and he examined all our records, of course, he would only take young men, he wouldn't take any old men ... it was a very cold voyage, and a pretty rough one and we had to take warm clothing ... and be prepared for very cold weather. We were ordered to be on board on Saturday at mid-day, because the tide was the afternoon.

We went down to Gravesend, and we anchored on what was called the Powder Ground, that's the ships loading explosives, had to be in a special anchorage away from the rest of the shipping. Quite a lump of explosives for the Hudson's Bay were loaded in the magazine. We went up through the north, right up to Peterhead in Scotland, I'll always remember that on the Monday was the date of the Coronation of King George V ... at noon that day, Captain had us all mustered to the cabin door and there issued a glass of rum to each man and we ... drank this to the health of King George V. When the wind was fair we stopped the main engines and went on as a sailing ship in order to conserve the coal ...

We would often go aloft just for sheer pleasure ... up the topsail yard and lean over the yard and there was a feeling of enormous pleasure and, we used to love it ... sit up there and lean over the yards and see the great sails below and you'd see the—the way the ship was surging away through the sea. We encountered icefields and ... then the sails had to be all furled and she had to proceed under steam through the ice packs.

... they brought a small bear on board destined for London Zoo ... and put him in ... into the henhouse! Well, of course, to us he was a great pet, he was only a small one, but we

Robert Williamson aboard the Discovery *on which he sailed from the West India Docks with ammunition and provisions for fur trappers at Hudson Bay in 1911. He was then nineteen years old.*

A rare and beautiful photograph from about 1870 of the riverside at Wapping. These sailing ships would have been in the coasting trade, bringing essential goods to London from various other parts of Britain. The barges or lighters were used to move cargoes around the port.

discovered he had a sweet tooth and that he liked burgoo for breakfast, that's the sailor's name for porridge. He was, naturally, of great interest to us. On the way home and in heavy weather he had a rather bad time being rolled around in his hen coop.

George Green, who is still a tugman on the Thames, can recall the days when the river was crammed with shipping:

If you can sort of imagine a large-scale Lord Mayor's procession which consisted of tugs of various sizes, dumb barges, sailing barges creeping up, the big ships with ship-towing tugs in attendance and the small ships making their own way up. And of course, lightermen driving their barges up by day and by night. Everyone working to their destinations on the flood.

Before the war was the most exciting time within the Port of London because almost everyone had a fair amount of skill. After the war you had the big motor tugs—the only person needing any skill was the tug master ... with six barges behind him he could wallop over the tide, under the tide any way he liked really. And now you come up and you're the lone survivor coming up from Sea Reach right the way through. If you meet anyone, well it's like a birthday party.

It might be said that the great historical question is not why the Thames in London has lost all this shipping, but how and why London's port had become of such international importance by the nineteenth century. For the Thames is not one of the world's physically

A classic riverscape from the 1880s. A steam tug tows a ship into the London docks past a sailing barge.

London was founded as a colonial outpost of the Roman Empire. On this medallion, found in France, the recapture of London is commemorated.

grand rivers like the Mississippi, the Nile or the Amazon. It is not even as long as the River Severn. All that can be said is that it was a big enough river to cope with the massive volume of trade which accumulated in London and which did not disappear until the 1970s.

The usefulness of a river like the Thames is obviously dependent on the sophistication of the society that exploits it. If we go back to a time before London was founded just under 2,000 years ago, the river is much more a natural barrier than a highway. Unembanked, the river spilt over marshes, and islands were formed at high tide where places like Bermondsey and Westminster were later built. At high tide, the Thames might have stretched a mile across where Westminster is now, running into creeks and pushing up the tributaries of the Thames, the Fleet, the Walbrook and other rivers long buried.

THE RISE AND FALL OF THE ROMAN PORT

It is clear from archaeological evidence that there were many settlements in the Thames Valley before the Romans arrived but there was nothing where the City of London is now. Medieval writers, anxious to give their city a grander tradition than it actually had, invented a pre-Roman Troy. But no modern archaeologist has found a trace of it. There was nothing there when Julius Caesar arrived in 55 BC to conquer the Britons. In Roman terms this was a primitive nation of tribes living in stick and mud houses.

Caesar did not sail up the Thames on the first available tide: he landed at Kent and marched north. He knew of the river and called it 'Tamesis'. Somewhere he crossed it, but his account of the invasion does not help to solve the argument now about where that was. The river is so changed it is doubtful if his description could ever be of much use. Some say it was across an ancient causeway at Westminster, which would line up with Edgware Road, formerly the Roman Watling Street. Others argue for Brentford, an established pre-Roman crossing and an easy place to ford. But it was almost certainly not, as many still believe, in the area of London Bridge. Caesar invaded twice, leaving in 54 BC, and there is no evidence that he had anything to do with establishing any kind of settlement at London. That occurred sometime between Caesar's departure and a further Roman invasion ninety years later.

The logic of building London, and establishing a port, arose out of the imposition of an imperial Roman pattern of settlement and trade

An imaginative, 'balloon' view of Roman London around AD 120, by the artist Alan Sorrell. Recent archaeological research has shown that the Thames was much wider and shallower when the Roman port flourished, and that when the Romans left this town its trade died. London disappeared for about 300 years after AD 410.

on Britain. Again, the invading armies were heading north from the Kent coast, and needed a crossing place on the Thames that would provide the most direct route to their principal town, Colchester. Although it has never been absolutely confirmed, it is generally believed that they built a wooden bridge across the Thames. There is much circumstantial evidence for this: the convergence of the roads from the south, more or less where London Bridge is now, and a concentration of Roman finds on either bank at that point. But exactly when it was built (if it was) we do not know.

There was great excitement in 1981 among archaeologists working on the Museum of London's 'rescue' excavation programme when they came across what might have been a pier of one of the Roman bridges. They were digging just ahead of the bulldozers on a site at Fish Street Hill and Lower Thames Street in the City. There was a first-century wooden wharf, part of the Roman port, and attached to it a structure that suggested by its arrangement of timbers that it might have been the base of a pier. It is indicative of how much the river and the City have changed since that time that the site was a long way north: well inland of the embankment and now the busy road.

A Japanese investment bank has since been built on the site, but other piers may emerge as excavations continue, with archaeologists working frantically in the foundations of City building sites. There is good reason to believe that this was the right place for the Romans to build a bridge. The Thames tides then probably turned around Westminster, so this was the furthest up-river the flood of sea water would carry ships from the channel. The low gravel hill on which St Paul's now stands would have provided firm standing for the northern part of the bridge, and possibly a sandy island in Southwark would have provided a base for southern piers.

The site was a junction for traffic coming north from the Kent coast, and shipping arriving on the Thames tides. The Romans created a thriving port here, principally on the north bank, and the range of archaeological finds is sufficient to suggest how their trade fluctuated over a period of four centuries. It is said they exported from Britain hunting dogs, skins and slaves. Their imports were exotic, and mostly from the Mediterranean, in the early years, becoming more localized later on.

It is really quite remarkable what the Romans hauled to Britain. From France, Spain, Italy and North Africa they brought in wine,

A clay figure from France, one of the early imports to London during the Roman period. This find was from New Fresh Wharf.

olive oil, grain, salt and preserved fish and fruit. Some was carried in pottery amphorae, and some in wooden barrels, the timbers of which were sometimes from trees in the Lebanon suggesting long-distance trade. Narbonne in southern France was the 'London' of the second and third centuries, gathering in Mediterranean trade and dispatching it along rivers to northern Europe. There was glassware from Italy, pottery from Spain and France, and even marble from Portugal. Millstones were brought in from Gaul and the Rhineland in the early period, despite the fact that they would have been available in Britain.

What seems to have happened, according to analyses of different finds which have been dated, is that as the Romans became established they relied less on imported goods and more on local goods. They began, in a way, the coasting trade, bringing in pottery from Dorset and ragstone from Kent. They got the east coast trade going with millstones and jet ornaments from York. Moreover, they started the up-river trade, bringing pottery down the Thames from Oxfordshire and Surrey.

As it had been founded by the Romans on a splendid river with its bridge and its evolving trade, you might imagine that London's importance grew steadily until it became the world's greatest City. But that is not so. In the earth beneath the City of London lies a great archaeological puzzle, only resolved to any satisfaction in the past ten years.

SAXON REVIVAL OF THE OLD PORT

The Romans left for good in AD 410, their empire collapsing. For the next four centuries, the earth beneath the City reveals few relics of any kind of settlement. Yet the Saxon chronicler Bede, writing in the eighth century but referring to an earlier period, describes Lundenwic as a lively international town by the standards of the day. The puzzle over what had happened to London in the intervening period began to be solved in 1988 when archaeologists found Saxon remains to the west of the Roman town, which had fallen into ruins. London really did not exist for maybe 200 years—the early Saxons did not live in towns—then began to re-emerge west of the old Roman City in the region of the Strand.

Over the next three centuries the Saxon kingdoms were once again divided by the river, and probably traded across it. Whatever there was in the way of a Roman bridge would have disappeared. The Thames was a barrier again. Some trade was carried up the river from

A glass flagon, probably imported from the Rhineland at the end of the Roman occupation of Britain.

Evidence of Roman London, an earthenware pot excavated on a site in Liverpool Street. Once the Romans had left Britain, there were few relics of any civilization in the district where this pot was found— the Saxons had moved upstream to the Aldwych.

Europe: millstones and Rhineland wine jars have been found in the area of the Strand. But this was more primitive than Roman culture and the Thames tides ebbed and flowed without much effect on trade.

When the Vikings began to attack the Thames estuary and Lundenvic in the ninth century the river, perhaps for the first time, provided the main highway for an invader. In 871–2 the Vikings spent the winter in London. The Saxons fought back, and finally King Alfred defeated them and re-established London inside the crumbling defensive walls of the old Roman town. That was 886. The former Saxon port became known as Aldwych—the Old Town. About a hundred or so years later a new bridge was probably built, again of wood, and the trade of the port expanded.

A tenth-century writer, Selfric, lists silks, precious stones, gold, wine, olive oil, ivory, bronze and glass among a merchant's goods. At Billingsgate, a Saxon wharf, custom duties were payable on timber, cloth, fish, chickens, eggs and dairy produce. Foreign merchants moved in to buy wool.

Then the Danes invaded, and for a brief period in the eleventh century Baltic amber, walrus-tusk ivory and whetstones from southern Norway feature in London's trade. In 1014, the Danish King Cnut ruled in London, but only briefly. When his son died in 1042 an English king, Ethelred, took over. It was in this period that Edward the Confessor helped to establish Westminster Abbey on an island where the River Tyburn ran into the Thames, on the site of a monastery. Christian missionaries had been arriving, with variable success, since the eighth century, converting kings, only to have rulers turn pagan again.

A new era began with the Norman conquest: Harold's defeat at Hastings, William's march to London, his surrounding of the town and its surrender, followed by his Coronation at Westminster on Christmas Day 1066.

Foreign merchants moved in again, from Rouen in France, and from the Rhineland. At the time, towards the end of the twelfth century, London had a population of perhaps 30,000. It was tiny in modern terms, and so undoubtedly was its trade. Thomas à Becket was the son of a Rouen merchant who had moved to London. He became Chancellor of England and Archbishop of Canterbury and, as is well known, was murdered in Canterbury Cathedral in 1170. His secretary, William Fitz-Stephen, who had seen him murdered, prefaced

The headquarters of what was to become the greatest of London's merchant companies whose wealth was founded on foreign trade. This woodcut shows East India House in 1648, half a century after the East India Company was formed.

a biography of the great man a few years later with an account of London, which all agree is a eulogy, but is not entirely fanciful. Even at that time he suggests the beginnings of a more considerable world trade in his verse:

The Arab sends gold, the Sabeen spice and incense,
The Scythian weapons; the fertile land of Babylon
Sends palm-oil from its rich forests, the Nile its precious stones,
The Chinese send purple dyed cloths, the French their wines,
The Norwegians and Russians send squirrel fur, miniver and
sables.

It was in this period that a momentous episode began, fixing firmly the position of the Port of London, and re-creating the great trading junctions of the Romans. This was the building of a stone bridge, one of the first of its kind in medieval Europe, across the Thames.

Old London Bridge, as it became known, was begun in 1176, and took more than thirty years to complete. It spanned the Thames on nineteen arches, supported by massive wooden starlings which acted as a breakwater to the tides, and effectively stopped all the large ships from going further inland. A drawbridge in the middle let ships

There was once a great ship-building industry on the Thames. All the chartered merchant companies were founded here, and the well-armed, ocean-going vessels of the East India Company were built at Deptford. This painting dates from about 1660.

A fifteenth-century ship taking passengers on board. This was long before England's fleet was a force to be reckoned with on the high seas.

through, at a price—there was a toll both under the bridge and over it—and there were wharves at Queenhithe for many years. But shipping and the port grew downstream, and London had captured the trade of the Thames.

At the time, nearly the whole of England's export was woollen cloth; eighty per cent going through London, and a tax on it helped to pay for the bridge. The taxing of trade became a great source of City wealth, the later coal tax not the least important.

But how and why did so much of the world's riches subsequently accumulate here, on the muddy banks of the Thames? The old schoolbook answer—that England, the nation of sea-dogs, developed an insuperable navy which made the world's oceans safe for the trade of its merchants and created an empire—will not do. There is some truth in it, however, and in so far as that heroic account does reflect historical reality, it is on the Thames that this great drama was played out.

Here the ships of the East India Company were built at Blackwall in the seventeenth century; downstream were the naval dockyards of Chatham; there were the royal palaces at Greenwich and Whitehall, Hampton Court and Windsor. And here was the great City of merchants who gambled their fortunes, and those of many a royal household, to fit out ships which set off to capture world trade from the middle of the sixteenth century.

The Russia Company began when three ships sailed from Ratcliffe, just below London Bridge, in 1553 carrying letters addressed to 'all kings, princes, rulers, judges, and governors of the earth'. They were searching for a northern route to the Indies, but the one surviving ship ended up on the Russian coast and the captain was introduced to Ivan the Terrible. Later, the Turkey, Levant, Africa, West India and—what was to be the greatest—East India Company were formed. All were begun by groups of merchants and members of the royal household in league with noblemen and with a royal charter to seek fortunes in all four corners of the world.

These charter companies and their ships were the exotic part of the Thames trade, representing the uneasy but profitable relationship between kings and queens, who needed money for wars and their opulent lifestyle, and merchants, who sought privileges. On the Thames, political and economic power sailed together, and often took to the river in their barges which were rowed by London watermen until the mid-nineteenth century.

An East Indiaman setting sail on a voyage which might take it three years to complete. The risks and rewards of foreign trade were great.

But this glamorous side of Thames trade, with all its pomp and its rich smell of gold and spices, was not necessarily the most important on the river, even in Elizabethan times. There was always a more mundane trade, which has had little attention from historians but is—arguably—the real key to London's wealth.

In Mayhew's description he mentions the colliers. These were the ships that brought the coal from the north-east coast—from Sunderland, Newcastle-upon-Tyne and some Scottish ports—to London by sea. They were part of a busy coastal trade that provided England in the seventeenth and eighteenth centuries with a great advantage over many of its European rivals in developing a national transport network. Down the east coast in sailing barges came corn, cheese, bacon, wet fish, and cloth. There was malt, bacon, horns, nails and beans from Hull and tin from Truro.

This was all carried in ships around the treacherous and stormy coast to the Thames, to sustain London. Whereas great European cities like Paris had to rely much more on river navigation (the Seine's tidal port is Rouen) and roads, England had a network of navigable tidal rivers which cut deep into the countryside and could link Norwich, or Cambridge, or York, or Lincoln with London by a sea route.

Windsor Castle in 1709 when river transport was essential for carrying goods and for communication with London. The great concentration of royal power on the Thames was important for the development of trade.

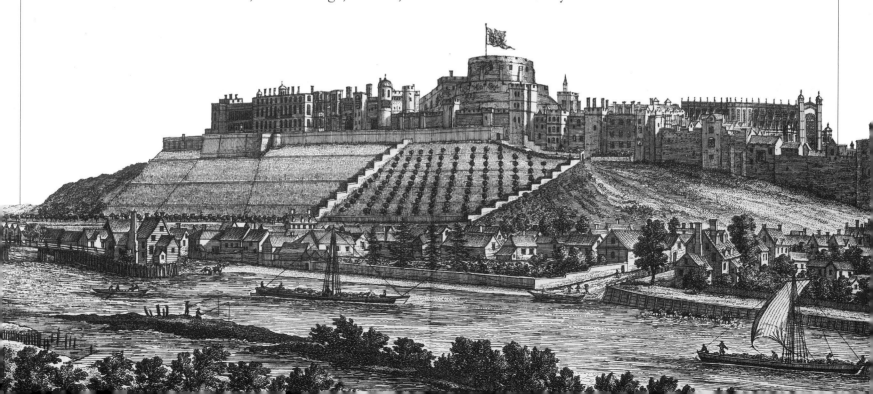

It was this advantage, in the days when roads were bad, before canals were cut in the eighteenth century, and before the railways, which gave England a great industrial lead and enabled London to grow as it did. The single most important trade in terms of bulk was that in coal, and by far the greatest traffic, as the old wreck charts of the east coast show, was between the river Tyne and London.

From the fourteenth century, when its import is first recorded, it was known as sea coal, to distinguish it from charcoal, which was also called simply coal. There is still an Old Sea Coal Lane which runs into Farringdon Road near Holborn Viaduct, and which would have been the site of a wharf here when the Fleet River was a tidal creek in which ships were moored. In the days of Drake and Raleigh, London was becoming dependent on coal for many of its industries and for domestic fuel.

It is very difficult to get excited about such a filthy black commodity as coal, and the claim that it was at the heart of London's prosperity might seem outlandish. But the point has been made by a number of historians. Was the English economy given its greatest boost first by domestic trade or by foreign trade? The importance of coal was pointed up nicely in a poem by John Cleveland in 1650:

> England's a perfect world, hath Indies too,
> Correct your maps, Newcastle is Peru.

A duty was paid on coal landed in London, and it was such a significant and easily available import that it was used to provide funds for re-building London after the Great Fire of 1666. St Paul's Cathedral, and many of the churches whose bells filled the air in Mayhew's description of the City, were financed out of a special tax on coal. This tax, which was levied in addition to other duties on coal, lasted from 1667 to 1889.

The coal was needed to sustain London from an early date because the town's houses and industries could no longer be fuelled with wood. It was a common domestic fuel in the days of Samuel Pepys who paid a very high price for it. When coal was in short supply because the collier ships had been attacked by pirates from Dunkirk, when civil war broke out, or when there was plague, or more commonly when the weather was bad, there was a crisis in London. The coastal trade kept London going from the sixteenth century until 1980, when the last of the power stations on the Thames within London closed down once and for all.

A wonderful illustration from about 1810 of the importance of the Thames as a lifeline for London's most basic needs: coal and building materials are being unloaded at the Adelphi Terrace (opposite). *Nearly everything came by river before the railways.*

An English armada that has been largely ignored by history, but was vital to London's prosperity—a collier (below) *coming from the north-east to the Thames around 1770.*

Trade cards of coal-merchants indicate the degree to which London had come to rely on coal for its heating and industries before the great age of steam. The card (above) dates from 1802, the other (below) from 1781.

Coal was important not only for fuelling London: the east coast collier fleet was a vital national resource. The collier ships of the eighteenth century and their crews were in great demand for the fitting out of the navy in times of war. The Press Gang was feared by the collier crews when they got news of war as they sailed up the Thames.

In 1724, Daniel Defoe, the author of *Robinson Crusoe*, in his *A Tour Through the Whole Island of Great Britain* reported:

> *I need not, except for the sake of strangers, take notice, that the City of London and parts adjacent, as also all the south of England is supplied with coals, called therefore sea coal, from Newcastle upon Tyne and from the coast of Durham and Northumberland … All these coals are bought and sold on this little spot of Room Land at Billingsgate and though sometimes, especially in case of a war or contrary winds, a fleet of five hundred to seven hundred sail of ships comes up the river at a time, yet they never want a market … This trade is so considerable it is esteemed a nursery of our best seamen.*

J. U. Nef, in his 1930s classic, *Rise of the British Coal Industry* has this to say about the coal trade:

> *When we add to the ships employed by the coal trade from Durham and Northumberland, the ships employed by that from Scottish and west-coast ports, it seems likely that, at the time of the Restoration, the tonnage of colliers had come to exceed the tonnage of all other British merchantmen. The coal trade from Newcastle to London was relatively no less important in the late seventeenth century, when, Adam Smith observes, it 'employs more shipping than all the carrying trades in England'.*

In the eighteenth century, many of the larger colliers were made at Whitby, the former whaling port of Yorkshire. It was here Captain James Cook learned his seamanship, and it was a converted Whitby collier, re-named the *Endeavour*, in which he set out on the first of his great expeditions. Whitby is recalled too in the name of one of London's most famous riverside pubs, the Prospect of Whitby. It dates from the sixteenth century, but was re-named the Prospect in the eighteenth century after a collier ship built in Whitby in 1777, and finally lost at sea in 1795.

In the history of shipping on the Thames, nothing has such a long span as the coal trade. Henry Mayhew gauged its significance in 1861, when the railways were beginning to take away some of the

trade. He reckoned there were 2,717 ships involved, carrying 3,418,000 tons of coal and employing 21,600 sailors. It looked then that this coasting trade would decline, but the arrival of steamships, which kept much better time, and then a new demand for coal from the gasworks and electricity generating stations, cement works, breweries and various other industries which became established on the Thames—as well as from steamships themselves—gave the colliers a welcome new lease of life. The railways handled domestic coal, the ships carried the industrial coal, which was the bulk of it from the turn of the century.

In both world wars the colliers were hammered by submarines—several companies lost nearly their whole fleet, and many of their men. They were easy prey on the east coast. London's coal supplies, as with so much else of its trade, had to be re-routed, ships were obliged to sail right round the north of Scotland and tugs had to go westwards instead of eastwards to pick up the goods brought in by railway and canal from the 'wrong side'.

During this century, the ships became bigger and the crews smaller, and a special kind of collier—the flat-iron or flattie—was designed to negotiate the seventeen bridges between Tower Bridge and the up-river gasworks and power stations at Wandsworth and Fulham. These ships ran so low in the water, and their decks were so washed over that they were sometimes nick-named the 'north-east submarines'.

Life aboard was pretty primitive, and within living memory the Geordie colliermen took with them a straw mattress to sleep on which they threw away after a few trips: it was known as the 'donkey's breakfast'. These coal ships still plied the Thames until the 1980s.

Kevin Greenwell worked as a steward on the colliers—a great contrast with life on the ocean liners:

> *I was a liner steward for eighteen years on the Cunard liners, besides that I went on the colliers. Colliers for me were a break, you could be back in the north-east in four days. That was the thing, getting back home and doing a bit of courting. But the price you had to pay was the conditions. They were very rough and ready. The* Firelight *must have been built in the Twenties, it had coal burners and coal-fired stoves so everything was bloody coal. Once you had everything washed down on the ship you could keep yourself clean for a couple days. I used to enjoy,*

When the American Ford Motor Company came to London in the 1930s, it chose a site on the Thames (left) where collier ships could supply its power station with coal. The rise of gas and electricity works ensured a continuing demand for coal in London until the 1980s—most of that for industry was brought up the Thames.

Gustav Doré's illustration of a coal wharf from around 1870. By that time, the railways had taken some trade away from shipping, but the coal traffic on the Thames picked up and increased later in the century.

One of a crew of just two men who together could sail a Thames sprit-sail barge, thus keeping costs competitive. The barges were the 'lorries' of the river, carrying low-value, bulk cargoes like hay, manure and grain.

you know, when you've got a storm brewing outside in your bunk, you've got Radio Luxembourg on and a mug of cocoa, my God, that was living.

As for uniforms, the officers did try, but if they did have gold braid, it was tatty. One skipper had the full number: white hat, scrambled egg on the peak. I thought, 'Bloody Hell, it's Jack Hawkins', and the nickname stuck. There was one first mate, I remember taking him a mug of cocoa on the bridge and there he is, bedroom slippers, white silk scarf, the full number, full-grown, fully-feathered seaman.

The very first time I went under Tower Bridge at night-time I stood on the after deck, in the middle there, about midnight, going under the bridge and looking up. And I could see the Tower was floodlit and when you're really down low it is terrific. The view is fantastic. That was a real buzz for me. I've seen New York, like you could dock at Manhattan at night-time and you've got the skyscrapers and the Chrysler building and the Empire State building, and I've climbed Table Mountain at Cape Town, but I always remember going under Tower Bridge, it was one of the things I enjoyed.

When I was back on the liners, on my way home from Southampton, nice tan, get a taxi over Waterloo Bridge, look down and see one of these bloody scruffy colliers, black hull, brown housing into the black background and the river. I used to think, Rather you than me mate!

As familiar on the Thames as the colliers were those evocative craft, the red-sailed sprit-sail barges. These were the workhorses or lorries of the river, carrying cheap, bulk cargoes from the east coast ports to London, and taking goods from foreign ships to towns along the estuary.

THAMES SAILING BARGES

The Thames sailing barge was tailor-made for the river. It was said they could sail wherever a duck could swim, as they were flat-bottomed, with no keel. 'Lee-boards', which hung like hinged fins from either side of the hull, prevented them drifing in the wind. Some of the larger barges would go out to sea, down to Cornwall to bring back china clay. Some would make trips to the continent, but most plied the Thames, supplying London with hay in the days of horse-drawn traffic and

An up-river barge (above) carrying goods from London to places like Reading and Maidenhead, painted in the late nineteenth century.

When London's transport was horse drawn, its essential fuel was hay which was brought in from Kent and Essex on sailing barges known as 'stackies' (left). A group of them is moored by Westminster in this painting from the late nineteenth century.

taking manure out. Most of the bargemen were not Londoners, but from the east coast. Dan Wills, a sailing bargeman for many years, recalls carrying manure down the river:

In London years ago there was as much traffic with horses as what there is today with motor cars and all the manure had to be collected up and it went all over Kent where we got all our best fruit. On the sailing barge we used to load manure. We'd have a kind of hole to let the steam out. You could smell some, but nothing to hurt and you was nice and warm at any rate. Course the manure used to warm up … it was a lovely smell. You know you'd think you was in the country on a farm when they was digging the manure out and putting it in the carts and it all used to get carted away up on to the farms.

What do you do when you are steering on the sailing barge? Wrap up. Keep your hands warm, have a pair of old socks. Put them on, stand at the wheel, you don't stand there rigid, not all the time, you are relaxed. When you walk to and fro, you have a look here and have a look there, so that everything's clear under the sail, go back and start steering again. In fact, you don't feel the cold so much on the barge as what you would ashore when you are walking around houses and you get draughts across your back, draughts from this way, that street, another street, and another. On the river you've got the wind one-way, the only time you get it bad, like sailing is if it's snowing or blowing and you sail into the wind.

A great deal of Thames trade was essential for London, but unglamorous. However, great riches did come from overseas, and it is to the development of this trade that we turn next.

Nobody has satisfactorily answered the question as to why London gained the dominance it did in both national and world affairs, but the vitality of its domestic, coal-based industrial economy, as well as its supremacy at sea, were significant factors. Which came first is a matter for argument.

When the coal economy was becoming established in the Elizabethan era, England was only just beginning to emerge as a major sea power. The country was not in the fifteenth century a nation of seadogs—in fact it never really was that. In the European shipping trade the Dutch were way ahead: they had, for example, 1,562 ships trading with the Baltic to England's fifty-one.

A satirical view of the Press Gang from the early nineteenth century when the navy relied in times of war on enforced recruitment. London's sailors and watermen were particularly vulnerable to the attentions of the Admiralty.

The Spanish and the Portugese were the great explorers and had opened the Americas and the Indies, but the Dutch, fighting to free themselves from Spanish domination, were defeated, and Antwerp, Euope's leading port and financial centre, was wiped out in 1576. Then, in 1588, the Spanish Armada was beaten back, by gales, fire ships and Drake's seamanship. It was touch and go though. England's merchant fleet then, on which the navy relied in time of war, had only just started to grow. It was founded on two things—the fishing industry, and the coal trade. Elizabeth I encouraged fishing by making Wednesdays as well as Fridays a day for eating fish, to encourage shipping and not, it was clearly stated, for 'superstitious' reasons.

While the Dutch and Spanish fought each other, the English nipped in and started working longer trade routes, increasing their shipping in the Mediterranean. And the merchant adventurer companies started out. England and the Thames were poised to make a great breakthrough. From Ratcliffe, little ships set out to seek new routes to the Indies: Sir Hugh Willoughby sailed from here in 1553 in search of the north-east passage. The first colonists of America also began their journeys on the Thames. Captain John Smith left from Blackwall in 1606 and established Jamestown Harbour, Virginia, the first permanent colony in the new world. In 1620, the *Mayflower* left from Rotherhithe under Captain Christopher Jones, before calling at Southampton and Plymouth on its way to America.

There was in London then a true sailortown in districts like Shadwell, Ratcliffe, Poplar and Wapping. It has been estimated that in 1650, about sixty per cent of grown men of Shadwell earned their living as seamen, lightermen and watermen, and another ten per cent from ship-building, boat-building and rigging.

It is really from the seventeenth century that it is possible to see London emerging as Europe's leading port, and to see why. Here was easily the greatest city in the British Isles, completely dominant, its people numbering maybe 200,000 in 1600 and rising to nearly half a million by the end of the century, when its nearest rival Norwich had a population of only 30,000. There is little doubt that this great concentration of wealth on the Thames was due to the historic appeal of the river to royalty and merchants alike.

Though enforced conscription into the forces became acceptable during this century, the less systematic operations of the navy's Press Gang were vilified in satirical works such as Gilray's 'The Liberty of the Subject'.

An astonishing panorama of London and the Thames painted around 1812, and only recently discovered. The significance of the river and shipping to the life of the metropolis is evident—nearly all the building materials and all the fuel to create this great city arrived on the Thames.

Even then, London was not simply a port—it was a great manufacturing centre of shoemakers, glovemakers, metal workers, goldsmiths and weavers, among others.

The River Thames, its tides a wonderful source of free power in the days of sailing ships, faced the continent from which most of the overseas trade came. A typical ship's load from Antwerp in 1567 had contained, according to the London port books, tennis balls, liquorice, silk made in Bruges, warming pans, thimbles and dyes for cloth. London became a great market, the demands of which affected the entire economy of the country.

More than any other European country, (with the exception of the Dutch), England had come to rely on its shipping for survival, and in time put more of its resources into the navy than the army.

In terms of sheer volume, the coasting trade probably outweighed the overseas cargoes until about the 1870s. The empire trade reached its zenith with the great steamships towards the turn of the century, by which time Britain controlled the single largest fleet in the world, and as a consequence was the greatest ship-builder of the time—though not on the Thames which had begun to lose that business to the north-east and Clydeside from the 1860s when iron ships began to predominate.

Within London, the port was probably losing dominance in the life of the town from as early as 1700, when it was thought about a quarter of the employed population were engaged in shipping. However, while declining in relative importance as an employer of London labour, the port grew steadily, extending eastwards towards down-river,

A great effort was made to rescue seamen in London (above) *from the clutches of 'crimps' who tried to cheat them of their earnings. This was the Sailors' Home and Red Ensign Club in the 1890s.*

A wonderful illustration of evangelists who took to the river to save the souls and lives of sailors. This is St Andrew's Waterside Church Mission (right).

its character constantly evolving. It became more and more separate from the rest of London, a world apart.

In the nineteenth century there was not one sailortown, but many. Out at the Victoria Dock it was reckoned that the local community and the seamen were closely related. They worked the steamships, kept on the coasting and continental runs, and had time at home. About a third of seamen docking there in the late nineteenth century actually lived in London. Another third were reckoned to have no home at all, anywhere in the world. These last were most prey to a seamy trade known generally as 'crimping'—the enticing of sailors into cheap lodging houses, getting them drunk and involved in prostitution.

The most notorious street for this in London was the Ratcliffe Highway just north of the London Docks. Here there were gin palaces, beer halls, all kinds of services to sailors, including brothels. The whole area of Ratcliffe, Wapping, Shadwell, Poplar and Limehouse was crawling with crimps of various kinds who sent runners to meet sailors off the ships to lure them in.

Most of the efforts to save seamen from this exploitation came from the missions that were set up in the area from the 1820s onwards. By the end of the century they had succeeded to a considerable extent in cleaning up sailortown by offering better, cheaper, alternative lodgings. The Sailors' Home in Well Street, near the London Docks, was set up as a charitable institution in 1835. In the 1850s it was boarding 5,000 seamen every year, while they waited for their next voyage. A report from the Home in 1854 set out the rival attractions of the area:

> *Within a few minutes' walk of the front door of the Sailors' Home are thirty licensed public houses (six of which are gin palaces) and also fourteen beer shops; in fact a beer shop or public house to every eight houses. Many of those public houses have long rooms attached to them, and in these places every inducement is held out to allure and entrap the sailor. At night, music, dancing, drinking and evil companions of both sexes are on the alert to keep him in a constant state of reckless excitement, and rob him of his hard-earned wages; and in the day-time these bars are filled and their doors thronged by the same parties engaged in the same nefarious pursuits.*

A change to both steamships and better cargo handling brought to the port a much quicker turn around: in the days of sail, when the old Pool of London was terribly congested, a seaman might be ashore for weeks. In the twentieth century it was more like days, and for the coastal trade it might be possible not to stay over in London at all. The flat-iron colliers with the right tides could unload at Fulham Power Station and go back out on the ebb tide. They used to hum to themselves a little ditty as they sped back up the east coast:

> *First the Dugeon then the Spurn*
> *Flamborough Head comes next on turn*
> *Whitby stands on high black land*
> *Forty miles from Sunderland.*
> *And so they say, if all gans reet,*
> *We'll be in canny Shields the neet.*

Riverside London remained a special kind of place in the 1930s, when the people of Wapping and Rotherhithe would gather on New Year's Eve for their own nautical celebration. A few minutes before midnight they would go down to the piers and quays and begin to sing. The river was crowded with ships from all over the world, colliers from the north-east, and the red-sailed Thames barges which plied between the Essex and Kent coasts and the riverside wharves. Tom Barett, a stevedore, remembers those days when he lived in Wapping:

> *New Year's Eve the whole of Wapping would wend their way*
> *down to Wapping Pier. Just before twelve o'clock, somebody*
> *would bang off with the song ... the bells were ringing the old*
> *year out ...*
>
> > *'I saw the old homestead*
> > *And faces I knew*
> > *I saw England's valleys and dells*
> > *I listened with joy*
> > *As I did when a boy*
> > *To the sound of the old village bells*
> > *The logs were burning brightly*
> > *For it's tonight that we banish all sins*
> > *For the bells were ringing the old year out*
> > *And the new year in.'*
>
> *And everybody'd go 'Yeahhhh!'. Then that would be twelve*
> *o'clock and all the ships, tugs, crafts would start blowing their*
> *sirens to the tempo of 'Happy New Year to all!' Tugs, ships,*
> *ringing their bells and their fo'c'sle heads and the whole caco-*
> *phony of this noise on the river was marvellous.*

The reading room of the Sailors' Home and Red Ensign Club in the 1920s. By that period, the work of Victorian philanthropists had cleaned up most of London's old sailortown.

DOCKLAND

CHAPTER 2

There has been a lament in recent years about the loss of London's Dockland, and many people find it distasteful that a region of the metropolis that once teemed with colourful life should be redeveloped now as marinas and high tech offices and the colour magazine crowd of fashionable media folk. Yet hardly anybody ever went to docklands, for it was made deliberately out of bounds to the people of London both by a fiercely proud working-class culture and a concern for security that the warehousing of valuable imported goods inevitably involved.

In the 1960s, the 'docker' was vilified in newspapers, and docklands thought of as synonymous with outmoded ways of working. Continuous strikes as the port workers grappled with what was to be the last struggle to retain some kind of livelihood in a way of life always governed by the uncertainty of trade and the continual obsolescence of shipping, made the docker a 'folk devil' of the age.

Now it is all smarmy sentimentalism about the richness of this riverside culture which grew up in a region of London which was vast and forbidding, and was only ever partially understood by anyone. What a shame the docks have gone and people are wind-surfing where once the fine ships of England's merchant fleet unloaded their sugar and tea, timber and whale oil, furs and ostrich feathers.

It is true that there is something surreal about the disappearance of such a cornucopia of activity in such a short space of time. How could it all disappear so fast? But, in a way, that has been the history of the Port of London for several centuries. Sudden fluctuations in trade were characteristic: an east wind would hold up the West India ships on their way to the brand new docks built to receive them on the Isle of Dogs in the early 1800s, and the small permanent staff of dockers would be put to mending roads in the Spring awaiting their arrival.

But the very idea of 'docklands' as a description of London's port is, in itself, misleading. Cargo docks are large areas of specially dug lagoons, connected to the river by locks, walled in and surrounded by warehouses. Long before any such docks existed, goods were unloaded in the Port of London. The creation of the docks, from 1802 onwards, was an attempt to cope with the increase in trade and to create more space for shipping; to keep up with the increase in the size of ships; to introduce new, mechanical ways of unloading ships; and to prevent pilfering on the river.

A magnificent and romanticized view of London's first great cargo docks built on the Isle of Dogs in 1802. This painting by William Daniell shows how far out of London the West India Docks were.

Whereas, from the first, Liverpool's docks were created by a public authority, London's were carved out by private enterprise. And it was private enterprise which continually undermined their profitability, for the dock companies competed not only with each other but with the owners of riverside warehousing who constantly took valuable trade away from the docks. A very large part of 'dockland' was in fact not docks at all. The big dock companies were drained of their profits by lightermen who had won the right to take goods off the ships in the docks and to paddle them out on to the Thames to be stored in riverside warehouses.

In this way London remained a river port, even though it had the largest system of enclosed docks in the world at the end of the nineteenth century. Recalling his first sight of London's port when he sailed up the Thames in the ship the *Duke of Sutherland* in October 1879, the novelist Joseph Conrad—a seaman before he began to write—recalled:

> This stretch of the Thames from London Bridge to the Albert Docks is to other watersides of river ports what a virgin forest would be to a garden. It is a thing grown up, not made. It recalls a jungle by the confused, varied, and impenetrable aspect of the buildings that line the shore, not according to a planned purpose, but as sprung up by accident from scattered seeds ... In other river ports it is not so. They lie open to their stream, with quays like broad clearings, with streets like avenues cut through thick timber for the convenience of trade. I am thinking now of river ports I have seen—of Antwerp, for instance, of Nantes or Bordeaux, or even old Rouen where the night watchmen of ships, elbows on rail, gaze at shop windows and brilliant cafés and see the audience go in and come out of the opera house. But London, the oldest and greatest of river ports, does not possess as much as a hundred yards of open quays upon its river front. Dark and impenetrable at night, like the face of a forest, is the London waterside.

This impenetrable region had grown up with a simple enough purpose: the loading and unloading of ships, the storage of their cargoes and their distribution around London and the country. But it was a jungle. No two cargoes were handled in quite the same way; no two docks had the same history, needs or working practices; the very term 'docker' is useless for understanding what went on by the riverside.

A classic dockland scene with lighters taking cargoes from the ships. Because lightermen had free access to the docks they could take goods out on to the Thames to be stored in riverside wharves. This kept the river busy but undermined the finances of the dock companies.

Sugar was a major import at the West India Docks. It was a rough cargo to handle, and the warehouse area in which it was unloaded was known as 'Blood Alley'. Here sugar sacks are hung out to dry.

The river itself and the miles of quays in the docks teemed with men—very few women worked in the port—performing an almost infinite variety of tasks in the Byzantine system, which, as Conrad says, had simply 'grown up'. The docker was only one of many port workers. He needs to be distinguished from the stevedore, who specialized in loading ships (the word is from the Spanish *estibador*, a packer), and the lighterman who moved goods around the docks in lighters or barges.

Dock work of all kinds was far more specialized and far more skilled than is often realized. Each cargo presented special problems, and the way in which ships were loaded and unloaded evolved over the years, as the design of ships and the nature of the docks changed. A vivid idea of the variety of work, and the physical toughness dockers needed is recorded in this account by Bill Reegan who started work in 1940. He went to the West India Docks, where a consignment of sugar had arrived at the North Quay then known as 'Blood Alley':

I started off with a great rush, I was a very fit young man at twenty-one, I don't think the middle-aged chap that I partnered was too impressed, but half-way through the morning, we'd had one bag or one sack of sugar that was torn and which showered all over us. I was perspiring, couldn't wipe it with a handkerchief because it was all gritty—it was in my hair down my neck … I wasn't at all pleased. And then as the morning wore on, holding the hook between the fingers of my right hand, the sugar particles rubbed off in between the fingers and that bled slightly. We went to lunch, I came back and was feeling rather weary, and about three o'clock in the afternoon I was praying for five o'clock to come so that I could climb up the steel ladder and go home out of it. About four-thirty approximately the ship worker and the top man appeared over the top of the hatch and shouted down, 'All night inside! Ship sailing.' I could have cried, we got a cup of tea and worked through to eight o'clock. I went home and mother put a meal in front of me, I told her I had to be back for eleven o'clock to work all night. I fell asleep half-way through the meal and she woke me up several times … I didn't have much to eat but I got back for eleven o'clock and then we were supposed to work through till seven the next morning. But we finished about six o'clock—no more cargo—but the treacle residue was all over the bottom of the ship's hold soaking into

The docker's hook was a feature of the overwhelmingly physical nature of work in London's port.

our boots. We came up out of there … I didn't know where I was, I cycled home, got to bed—and oh we had the next day off—I think I slept most of the day I could hardly get out of bed in the afternoon I was so stiff, and that was my story of the first day of work.

Alex Gander, now in his eighties, worked in many different parts of the docks over forty years:

Bags of talcum powder, that was a hard slippery job, you couldn't grip the bags and another rotten job was on the iodine, you had to tear the lids off the small kegs, shake the iodine out on the floor, weigh it and then put it back. Well the whole warehouse was yellow … the walls were yellow and you can guess what the men's throats were like and clothes. Some men couldn't do the job but some who did it regularly had scabs on their wrists … that was through the iodine. But after the war the young fellows wouldn't stand for it, they demanded milk and to do the job in the open air. Another rotten job was on the skins where the skins would come up—horses' skins, cattle skins and they'd have bands round them and you'd have to chop the bands like we used to chop the bales of wool and they'd all spring up in the air. There was dog skins—we are supposed to be animal lovers, but there was about a thousand dogs a day killed in London and they come up in bags … all wet bags, mangy skinny dirty dogs all wet and blood and you'd have to handle these bags without any protective clothing and they would go to the continent where they tell me that they were made into chamois leather gloves.

One of the tea jobs in the warehouses in Wapping and in the London Dock was blending—if a company wanted a certain blend you'd have to turn, say, ten chests of Assam tea on to the floor and you had big flat shovels which you threw in the air and you can guess the state you were in after doing that: it'd be in your eyes, your ears, nose, throat, down your neck and then it would have to be put back into the chests at the same weight that was marked on the chest.

If it wasn't the same weight as you wanted it, you'd have to shoot it all out again and do it again. Well the toilets in the St Katherine Dock especially were awful and you'd be down there and your boots would be sodden with urine and you'd come back and tread the tea in.

To keep down their costs the commercial dock companies relied on cheap, casual labour for the unloading of ships. The men were hired by the day, or half-day, and often fought for the right to work at the notorious 'call on' at the dock gates. This was the scene at the West India Docks in 1886.

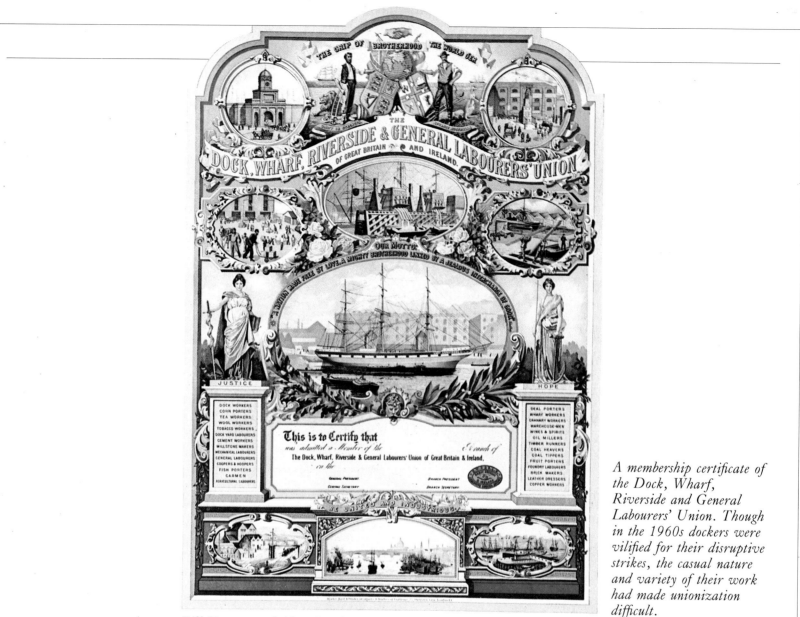

A membership certificate of the Dock, Wharf, Riverside and General Labourers' Union. Though in the 1960s dockers were vilified for their disruptive strikes, the casual nature and variety of their work had made unionization difficult.

Bill Reegan and Alex Gander were casual dockers who, before the last war, gathered at the dock gates for the call on, a primitive scramble for work. After the war, the Dock Labour Scheme did away with the call on and attempted to give registered dockers regular work. But it had not been long in operation when the port began to disappear from London and was transformed by containerism.

The great army of casual dock workers was the creation of the nineteenth century. Before the docks were built, an ancient and relatively

Before the docks were built, all goods that were subject to customs dues —the great majority—had to be landed at legal quays. This was Custom House quay in the eighteenth century.

well-ordered practice for the loading and unloading of ships had grown up. It broke down because the old river port could not cope with the increase in trade in the eighteenth century.

FORERUNNERS OF THE DOCKER

From the late Middle Ages, City merchants had had the problem of finding people to handle their cargoes. It was rough work, but the merchandise was valuable, and they wanted reliable men. A practice arose by which the merchant companies employed porters who had to establish their 'good character' and belong to an organization.

There were the Tacklehouse porters, who worked for one of the twelve livery companies in the City. There were the ticket porters, the fellowship porters and the aliens porters. All of these groups, which by the eighteenth century were well-organized, had a history of association with a particular branch of trade, and special functions. They were often warehousemen as well as porters.

For example, the Tacklehouse porters of the Vintners Company had in 1508 the sole right to deal with wines imported to the City. In the latter half of the sixteenth century, the Tacklehouse porters were also working for the Haberdashers, who imported wool from Spain, the Grocers, Salters and Fishmongers. By the eighteenth century they operated almost like guilds, and to become a Tacklehouse porter you had to put up a surety of £500 with four householders as referees. By that time Tacklehouse porters had come to specialize in the goods from the South Sea Company, the East India Company, Ireland, coastal trade and British plantations. Ticket porters had a monopoly of work with pitch, tar, deals, flax, hemp and various Baltic goods, as well as other categories, and worked under the Tacklehouse porters. Fellowship porters dealt in corn, coal and salt and all those things that could be measured in dry weight. Alien porters were responsible for carrying the goods of foreign merchants.

Over the centuries there were many disputes and accusations of sharp practices, as you would expect in this line of business, but by and large the porterage system was closely organized and evolved to deal with new conditions and new kinds of cargo. It became especially important that the unloading of goods should be regulated for many of them carried a duty collected at the port. From Elizabethan times, 'legal quays' were established at which any dutiable goods had to be landed. At first these were all on the north bank, the City's waterfront,

A graphic illustration of the richness of London's riverside activity—the wharves below London Bridge.

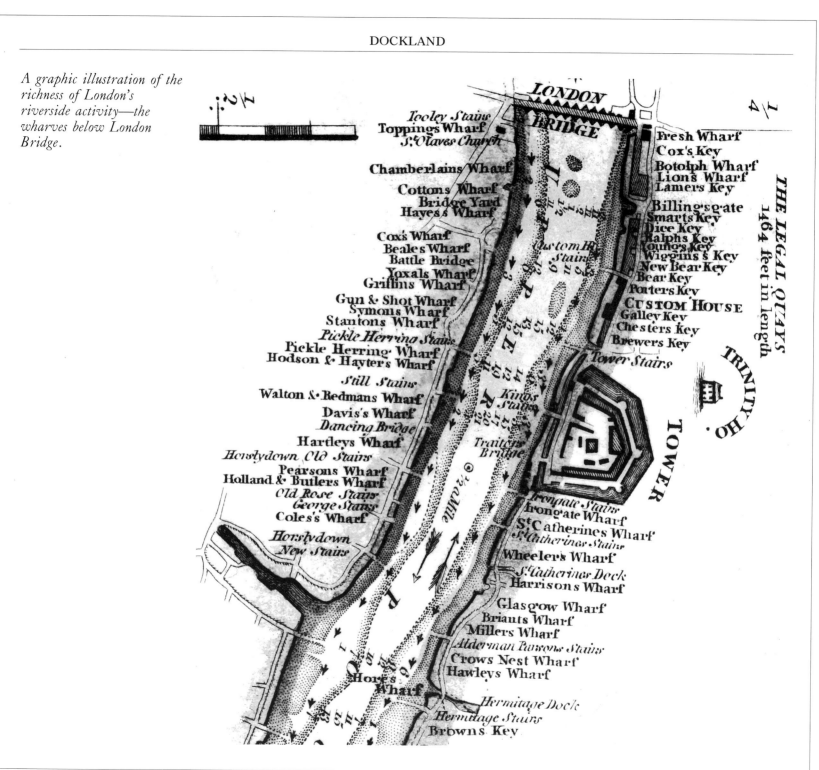

A wonderful portrayal of the Thames lightermen at work at the turn of the century by the painter William Wyllie. The angle at which the man is rowing looks fanciful, but it is accurate. The 'dumb' barge, or lighter, was powered by the tide, and steered with great oars.

but pressure for more space led to the establishment of 'sufferance wharves' on the south bank to provide more extensive quays and warehousing for these goods.

Some idea of the status of porters and their relationship with merchants is indicated by a colourful ritual the ticket porters had each year. These porters would attend a sermon on the Sunday after 29 June at St Mary at Hill Church. On the night before they would present nosegays—little bouquets of flowers—to the merchants living near Billingsgate. At the service, porters, merchants, their wives and children all carried nosegays and gave gifts for the relief of the poor.

The watermen and lightermen on the Thames—the river was administered then by the City Corporation—had their company, with a system of apprenticeship and an entrance fee. Although their skills were regarded as the same, watermen carried passengers, while lightermen carried goods. Both acted as pilots on the river, and were regarded as having a specialist knowledge of the 'set' of the tides, as they do today.

This crammed and relatively intimate world of London's port had, inevitably, to come to an end as the trade of the port increased. It was impossible for it to extend up-river, beyond Old London Bridge, without knocking that bridge down. In any case, ships were getting larger, and the river was becoming silted up. An empty ship had to take on ballast for its stability—a weight of sand and gravel—and much of this was thrown into the river by vessels arriving unladen. Although there were ballast lighters collecting the sand and gravel to load into empty ships leaving the port—such as colliers bound for the north-east—they did nothing to clear mud-banks which formed in the river because mud was not saleable as ballast. The river was silting up and congestion in the port was chronic. Sailing ships often arrived *en masse* when the wind was favourable, and much of the trade was seasonal anyway. At crowded times it was sometimes impossible to cross the river with a lighter, and ships had to wait for weeks for an opportunity to unload. All the time the amount of shipping was increasing. In 1794, 3,663 ships came into the port—2,500 more than at the start of the century. The quays could become crammed with hogsheads of sugar, brought in by convoys of ships and stacked waiting to be checked and for customs dues to be paid. The crowding and confusion was made worse by the fact that merchants had taken to trading on the quays, which became impromptu market places.

Finally, there was the problem of crime. A colourful array of specialists at removing cargo, which lay on the river awaiting unloading, arose in the port, each with his own technique and name.

A committee of the House of Commons formed in 1796 to consider reform of the port heard about the activities of 'river pirates' who cut lighters adrift then pillaged their goods downstream; watermen who were 'night plunderers'; 'scuffle hunters' scavenging on the quays; 'light horsemen' who were mates on ships or revenue officers in league with them; 'heavy horsemen' who were porters and labourers wearing baggy clothing to conceal stolen goods; and 'mud-larks' who threw goods overboard at high tide so that they could be collected from the mud at low tide. It was thought this plunder cost between £250,000 and £800,000 a year: a tiny fraction of the value of all goods, but worrying for the merchants.

An attempt to stamp out this crime in the handling of West India cargoes of sugar and rum was made just before the first docks were built. A Scotsman, Patrick Colquhoun, who had been in the cotton trade and had lived in Virginia, North America, settled in London. He became a magistrate in Wapping and wrote a report on crime on the river. In 1798 he formed a small police force with a magistrate, a clerk, a chief constable and a force of armed men. It is appropriate that London's first organized police force—the Bow Street Runners were rather different—should have been formed to combat pillage in the port, for that is where the great concentration of goods lay. Colquhoun's influence on the West India merchants also led to a new regime in handling their goods, with the labourers forced to abandon their suspiciously baggy clothing and to wear stockings and breeches.

London's earliest docks were for ship-building, not for the landing and loading of cargoes. This was the Blackwall Yard around 1770 (above and opposite).

But this did nothing to improve the workings of the port, and it became clear that the only solution was to start building docks. Many schemes were considered by the Commons committee, but there was no overall planning for the port—simply competing economic interests.

Naturally, the traditional port workers—the Tacklehouse and ticket porters—were against the docks, as were the owners of legal quays (who saw themselves losing business), and many with interests in the City. But the merchants had an inevitable logic on their side, and Acts of Parliament were passed allowing for the creation of the docks, and offering compensation for those who would lose out.

It was the West India merchants who created the first dock. They chose a site out to the east in the countryside, on the northern part of a marshy peninsula which had been fortified against Thames tides and drained by Dutch engineers. This was the Isle of Dogs, the name probably a corruption of Dutch *dijks* or dykes, meaning a drainage ditch.

Part of the reason for building here was the cheapness of land compared with the built-up areas nearer London. It was also possible for the relatively large West India vessels to come off the river well below London Bridge. At one time the City had had a scheme for cutting a canal across the north of the Isle of Dogs to shorten the journey up to London. The City got involved with the West India Docks scheme by financing the building of a canal connecting the huge parallel dock area with Blackwall. Ships came off the Thames at high tide into the dock basin. The lock gates were closed, and they then moved in alongside the quays. Goods unloaded into lighters could leave the docks from the other end, take the canal through to the Thames on the other side of the Isle of Dogs and head for the Port of London.

To defray the enormous cost of the docks, which were opened with much pomp in 1802, they were given a twenty-one-year monopoly on West India trade.

Next in the wave of early nineteenth-century dock building was a vast area carved out of the old sailortown of Wapping, much nearer the City than the West India Docks. Again there was massive opposition from the vested interests. Once more, the City, while opposing the scheme, got financially involved. The old porters' organizations were excluded.

Enormous sums had to be paid out in compensation to those who lost their homes and business, and to the Shadwell Waterworks (see chapter 5), which the London Dock Company bought out as the building of the docks were said to interfere with its water supply which came principally from the Thames.

The first ship entered the new London docks on 31 January 1805. For twenty-one years the London Dock had the monopoly on all ships coming to London with tobacco, rice, wine and brandy—except those already cornered by the East India trade.

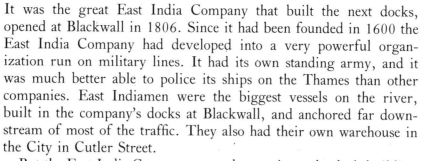

It was the great East India Company that built the next docks, opened at Blackwall in 1806. Since it had been founded in 1600 the East India Company had developed into a very powerful organization run on military lines. It had its own standing army, and it was much better able to police its ships on the Thames than other companies. East Indiamen were the biggest vessels on the river, built in the company's docks at Blackwall, and anchored far downstream of most of the traffic. They also had their own warehouse in the City in Cutler Street.

But the East India Company wanted to get in on the dock-building mania, and took over an area on the Isle of Dogs where there was an old eighteenth-century dock, and dug out a massive new system.

South of the river, the Grand Surrey Canal Company, with a scheme to bring in market garden produce from Kent, proposed the creation of a dock linking the canal and the Thames. There were other schemes—to link London and Portsmouth by canal, for example. The Surrey canal got as far as Peckham and stopped. Other dock-building schemes in the Rotherhithe area were put forward: it was a shambles.

There were long-established docks in the area, which had been used—like the East India Docks at Blackwall—for fitting out and repairing ships. There was the Howland great wet dock, and the Greenland Dock dating from London's importance as a whaling centre. These old docks and the new docks were turned, by a series of schemes and amalgamations, into the Surrey Commercial Dock system. In his book, *History of the Port of London*, written in the 1920s, Sir Joseph Broodbank has this to say of the Surrey Docks:

> *The system, which consists of nine docks, six timber ponds, and a canal three and a half miles long, extending to Peckham, originally formed the property of four companies ... Each company built its accommodation as suited the requirements of its customers at the moment ... No worse case can be found of the results of competitive individual interests being allowed to cater for public requirements.*

The Surrey Docks came to specialize in corn and timber, and were amongst the last to modernize their handling of goods. It was known always as a 'stevedores' dock—they monopolized it—and was famous until recent times for its 'deal porters', men who carried on their shoulders what seemed to be impossible loads of timber which they stacked on the quaysides.

The building of St Katherine's Dock in the 1820s. Thousands of people were made homeless as the old sailortown of London was cleared for the new dock.

Two young lightermen with their barge in 1946. Though steamtugs replaced much of the work of the rowed or 'driven' barge, there were still some on the river in the 1970s.

If the Surrey Docks were an administrative mess, then the next great dock to be built was easily the most contentious. Today, St Katherine's Dock, refurbished as a tourist centre, appears quaint and attractive—a piece of historic London to be saved from the voracious City developers. When it was carved out of a heavily populated part of London in the 1820s it was regarded widely as an act of terrible vandalism. No less than 11,300 people were evicted, only those of any substance receiving compensation. The rest moved out from mean streets called Dark Entry, Cat's Hole, Shovel Alley, Rookery and Pillory Lane.

The various interests—merchants, shipowners and investors— hoped to make a killing because the other docks were about to lose their twenty-one-year monopolies on trade. Their dock would be right next to the City, with warehouses on to the quay so that cargoes could be unloaded from ship to warehouse floor. Carved out as it was from a built-up area, this was smaller than the other dock systems, a factor which hampered its operation almost as soon as it was opened in 1828. It was named after the most celebrated building it did away with, the St Katherine's Hospital, founded 700 years earlier. There was a great outcry about its removal, but those running it accepted an offer of alternative and more modern premises by Regent's Park, which was just then being laid out by the architect John Nash.

Thus it came about that London's newest dock was closest to the City and its oldest dock furthest away, the reverse of what might have been expected, and still a cause of confusion for tourists who reasonably think of St Katherine's as the original.

It was the intention, as is invariably the case when great new schemes are pushed through, to 'modernize' the handling of cargo in the port, and to do away with the pilfering so commonplace on the river. The docks therefore had twenty-foot-high walls, a police force who could search those working in the docks at the end of the day, and a rule that nobody could leave the docks in working hours. They were a fortress, with some of the dock workers armed as a militia in the early days. The City porters were excluded from working there.

However, a 'freewater' clause was included in the West India Dock Act which allowed lightermen in and out of the new docks without paying any charge. All the other new docks had the same clause. While the dock companies' monopoly on goods lasted, it did not mean much, and watermen and lightermen were compensated for loss of

Barges at work at a dock entrance, painted by Thomas Shepherd in 1825.

work as part of the deal in building the docks. However, once the monopolies had expired, the lightermen came back into the docks and took the warehousing trade away from the dock companies. This was a serious loss, for the West India Docks were lined with miles of warehousing and a large part of their income was to come from the charges they made. The freewater clause of the lightermen kept cargoes moving about on the river, from docks to wharves. This aspect of the port was one of its most extraordinary features, which survived until the modern era.

The barge or lighter is quite a large vessel with no motor or sail. It can only be moved by the force of the tide. A lighterman can merely steer the barge using enormously long oars. Until tugs towing lighters appeared, it was with these powerless or 'dumb' barges that a great deal of the cargo of London's port was moved about. Right up to the present day, the basic skill of the lightermen is to know the intricacies of the 'set' of the tides in the Thames, as the force of water bounces from bank to bank, and there is no better way to learn about the river than in a dumb barge. Bob Harris remembers his first trip after his apprenticeship:

One could never forget the first drive under oars, rowing under oars is called driving, and on the first drive, from a boy one suddenly becomes a man.

And it was traditional then that a tug skipper, if he'd had a boy who'd been with him he would give him a start because there is a saying on the river, 'A bad tow is better than a good row.' And as Arthur Hudson came up, he said, 'Take my line, Bob, where're you going?' So I said, 'I'm going up to Morton's Wharf.' 'Oh I'll take you up,' he said. I said, 'You can't take me right up there Arthur.' 'OK,' he said, 'I'll let you go then at Millwall Dock.' Well, Millwall Dock is only about quarter of a mile away from Morton's Wharf and no one can see me on the tug. So I shoved off there, but shot off his tug with far too much way and went crashing into the barge roads with the tide slopping up.

I had to stay where I was until just half an hour before high water ... when I poked her out I rowed feverishly up to the wharf and I can see the men now, looking at their watches as I rowed in. And they all knew that something had happened ... no one said anything, but they knew that something had happened—I done something that I shouldn't have done ... People on the river don't like being embarrassed and if ever you see a tug gone aground you'll never see a member of the crew—it's a bit like the Marie Céleste—*no one will ever know.*

Lightermen were the élite labour force in the port. They were employed by firms of master-lightermen, and were always very proud of their skills and their knowledge of the river. At the end of the nineteenth century their quaintness on the Thames was not appreciated by everybody. In his guidebook, *Dickens's Dictionary of the Thames*, Charles Dickens regarded them as absurd. He had the tourist perspective on things, and was concerned that the lightermen got in the way of pleasure steamers. He quotes a traffic committee which had just reported to the effect that dumb barges clogged up the river.

The only use of the long sweeps [oars] with which they are provided is, in fact, to keep the barge straight, and even this is difficult, if not impossible, in a high wind. They are quite incapable of getting out of the way, or keeping a definite course, and as they bump about among the shipping and get across the bows of steamers, they are the very type of blundering obstructiveness, and an excellent example of how time is allowed to be wasted in this country.

At the time this was written in the latter half of the nineteenth century the number of lightermen was beginning to increase on the Thames

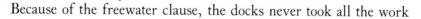

below London Bridge. Watermen, who carried passengers, were just disappearing (see next chapter) and were becoming lightermen as the quantity of cargo handled in the Port of London continued to grow. Steamtugs pulling a string of barges were common by then, but they were less flexible in the way they distributed cargo than a single lighter which could go more easily from one wharf to another with a variety of goods to deliver or pick up. Lightermen, whether skippering tugs which towed barges or 'driving' dumb barges, survived until the end of the life of the port in London. The few remaining tugs are worked by them, as are the pleasure boats on the Thames.

Because of the freewater clause, the docks never took all the work

The busy riverside wharves and warehouses by Southwark Bridge as it was in 1819.

away from the river. In fact it was evident after half a century of frenetic dock building that many of the problems they were supposed to solve remained. The number of ships moored in the Pool of London and on the river increased from 8,000 in 1808 to 16,000 in 1824.

When Mayhew was writing in the 1850s most of the river characters the docks were built to exclude were still trying to eke out a living stealing from boats, and the nature of dock work had hardly changed at all. The former Tacklehouse and ticket porters were on their way out, and the casual docker was becoming much more common. Stevedores had developed as a strongly clannish group dominated by the Irish who had been arriving since the eighteenth century, and were valued for their strength which was also appreciated in canal digging—the 'navvies' or navigators—and later in road building. An enormous influx of Irish followed the great famine of the 1840s, and right up to the last days of the docks, stevedores were the descendants of these families, speaking with London accents but proudly preserving their Irish heritage and names. They kept themselves apart, were not controlled by the dock companies, and like the lightermen organized themselves into contracting firms. They were also the first group of dock workers to become unionized in the modern sense. Crudely speaking, dock work had changed its character, the porter fraternities were broken, and a great army of casual labourers and better organized and better paid stevedores had emerged.

Under a heading 'Felonies on the River Thames', Mayhew lists in *London Labour and the London Poor*, among other well-known scavengers, mud-larks, sweeping boys, sellers of small wares, river pirates and dredgermen. The mud-larks were often children who collected coal in the river that had spilled from barges—with their help:

> In the neighbourhood of Blackfriars Bridge mud-larks of various ages may be seen from ten to fifty years, young girls and old women as well as boys. They are mostly at work along the coal wharves where the barges are lying aground, such as Shadwell and Wapping, along Bankside, Borough; above Waterloo Bridge, and from the Temple down to St Paul's wharf.

Dredgermen trawled the river bed for spilled coal and Mayhew thought they were probably descended from Thames fishermen who used to make a living picking up drowned bodies, particularly from accidents in 'shooting' Old London Bridge. Most of the other 'thieves' had a ruse to get on a boat at night, pretending they were selling

Riverside people—keepers of the Falcon Dock, the Edwards family, in 1923.

something or they were seamen, and robbing the boat of some of its cargo or rope. Mayhew cites a court case in which two chimney sweeps were stopped by river police while rowing away from a ship and were caught with a haul of tobacco concealed under a mound of soot.

The amount and variety of work that remained on the river is illustrated by Mayhew's description of the itinerant beer sellers of the port, the 'purl-men'. These served sailors on corn, coal and timber ships, lumpers unloading timber from ships; ballast heavers, ballast getters, corn porters, coal whippers, watermen (taking passengers from ship to shore) and lightermen. The purl-man would have a broad skiff which would not tip over in the wash of the steam-boats in the port:

> *Thus equipped he then goes to some of the small breweries, where he gets two 'pins' or small casks of beer ... after this he furnishes himself with a quart or two of gin from some publican, which he carries in a tin vessel with a long neck, like a bottle —an iron or tin vessel to hold the fire, with holes drilled all round to admit the air and keep the fuel burning, and a huge bell, by no means the least important portion of his fit out ... with his tin gin bottle close to his hand beneath the seat ... and his fire pan secured on the bottom of his boat, and sending up a black smoke he takes his seat early in the morning and pulls away from the shore, resting now and then on his oars, to ring the heavy bell that announces his approach. Those on board the vessels requiring refreshment, when they hear the bell, hail, 'Purl ahoy!'*

Not only had the river retained a great deal of work, the coming of the docks had done little to alleviate the fearful nature of the physical work involved. The most exhausting job was probably that of coal-whipper.

A gang of these men would be engaged at a certain rate to unload a coal ship or barge. There were nine men in a gang: three would be in the hold loading a basket which was suspended on a rope. The rope was thrown over a crude kind of wooden frame, and other gang members would climb the frame and take an end of the rope. They could not see into the hold, but could tell you when the basket was full. At that point they hauled the basket up and, jumping down from the frame simultaneously, their combined weight would lift it so that another gang member could swing the basket and tip it to unload the coal. Mayhew records:

> *Sailors when they pull away together generally time their pulling to some rude chant ... The coal-whippers do their work in*

A gang of coal-whippers at work unloading a ship on the Thames. Four men use their combined weight to raise a basket full of coal which is tipped into a lighter.

perfect silence: they do it indeed like work and hard work too. The basket-man and the meter [measuring the coal] are equally silent, so that nothing is heard but the friction of the ropes, and the discharging of coal from the basket into the machine, and from the machine into the barge. The usual amount of work done by the whippers in a day ... is to unload, or whip, ninety-eight tons! To whip one ton, these men jump up and down 144 feet ... [they] therefore raise 1½ cwt. nearly four miles high.

The coal-whippers' basket is the centrepiece of this demonstration during the first great dock strike in 1889. In the City there was great support for the dock workers.

Mayhew reckoned there were 200 gangs of coal-whippers. Although their work was getting better regulated, they were for years dependent on publicans to find them jobs, and Mayhew believed these publicans were the relatives of northern ship owners.

Throughout their history, the men who worked in the port hung on to ancient practices because innovation in the form of powered cranes and winches meant that they lost their jobs, however tough those jobs were. The dock companies generally encouraged this in the nineteenth century because the competition between them, as well as their own incompetence on many occasions, meant that they were always looking for ways to save money. The easiest way to do this was to reduce the price of the cheapest form of power available, which was poverty-stricken men.

With the river still crowded with ships, steamers becoming more common, and the first docks struggling to survive, a new spate of dock building began in the 1850s.

In 1855 Prince Albert opened the Victoria Docks, the furthest downstream, and promoted by railway interests. It was built for steamers, had a railway link with London, and hydraulic lifting gear. In 1864 the Millwall Dock was opened on the Isle of Dogs with the intention of developing industry on the surplus land around. It took grain from the Baltic, but it was a financial failure from the start. The South West India Dock was opened in 1870, designed to store enormous quantities of goods at a time when steamships and railways made the fast movement of cargoes much easier. Because the larger steamers were very expensive it was necessary for them to 'turn around' quickly. Earlier dock companies amalgamated. And then in 1866, the East and West India Dock Company built

A superb aerial view (opposite) of the riverside wharves and dockland towards the end of their life. In the foreground, St Katherine's Dock by Tower Bridge is closed, but the London Dock just beyond is working, as are the Surrey Docks south of the river and the West India Docks on the opposite bank. In the far distance are the Royal Docks.

brand new Tilbury Dock out on the Essex marshes, twenty-six miles from London.

It began badly at Tilbury. The lightermen would not go that far down, shipping companies had been encouraged by other dock companies not to go there, and the wharfingers higher up the river boycotted Tilbury goods. Between April and August 1886, a line of German steamers from Central America were the only customers of note. So

Tilbury reduced its rates for docking, and seduced shipping companies away from the established Albert and West India Docks, whose dividends fell, and the competitive spiral downwards once again undermined the economies of the dock companies.

To save money, the companies cut the rates of dockers and encouraged the swelling of the hordes of casual labourers who went to the call on each morning in the hope of a few hours' work. They might be engaged for just one hour and paid off. In 1889, the celebrated strike in the docks spread like wildfire amongst an otherwise ill-organized mass of men, who demanded 6d. an hour—the 'docker's tanner'—and a minimum half-day hiring. It was an extraordinary strike, which had massive public support, and was marked by orderly marches through the City by dock workers. It began with a relatively small group of workers, not all of them dockers: they belonged to the Tea Operatives Union, worked in warehouses in Wapping and were led by Ben Tillet; and also the Gasworkers Union formed at Beckton Gas Works—then the largest in the world—led by Will Thorne. The lightermen and stevedores gave their backing, and the docks closed down for a month, despite the imports of black-leg labour. Public donations to support the strikers, who would have had no savings, were vital for the success of the action, and donations, thought to have totalled £24,000, from Australian dock workers ensured that the men held out.

City people and merchants who wanted their goods shifted had little sympathy with the financially inept dock companies which were seen as the villain of the piece. It was the first major dock strike, and the last one in which the dockers could count on such whole-hearted support from the public at large.

The ailing dock companies were finally abolished—just as private enterprise water companies, and later transport and coal mining companies were done away with—in 1908. This was not for any overtly 'socialist' reasons, although some at the time thought such a move revolutionary. It was simply that the private companies had made a mess of the extremely difficult problem of enlarging London's port as the scale and the nature of trade increased in the nineteenth century.

The Port of London Authority (PLA) came into being in 1909, with a splendid new headquarters in the City, and set about making some kind of sense of the hopeless and by then gigantic wilderness of the London docks, which stretched for miles to the east of London and beyond. This was in the early days of film, and from the 1920s the

Ostrich feathers, on show at the Cutler Street warehouse, were a characteristic luxury from abroad.

Notice of a sale of exotic feathers in the City when plumage was fashionable for ladies' dresses as well as for ceremonial wear. The 'osprey' feathers were probably not those of the recently re-introduced fish eagle, but egret feathers from abroad.

PLA tried to improve the image of docklands by making many promotional documentaries, mostly emphasizing the modern equipment they had installed in the 'Royals', Victoria and Albert, and their own new dock, the George V, built below the Albert, and opened in July 1921. However, the PLA did not end the trouble in the docks, and it had to face the shutdown of the general strike for ten days in 1926, when the troops were drafted in to unload cargoes and submarines appeared in the brand new George V Dock to provide a floating supply of electricity.

LOOKING FOR WORK

In the 1930s, the dockers' call on still existed, the wharves on the river continued to handle a great deal of the storing of goods, and the river remained crammed with ships. Jack Banfield, who as a young man had been to sea, joined the army of casual labourers in the 1930s. He lived in Wapping and, like many of the dockers there, evolved his own way of spying for work each morning before he made the contacts which gave him more regular work:

In the mornings I'd leave home about half past six and on many occasions I'd go on to Tower Bridge and I'd get there about seven o'clock and I'd look each side of the river, the south side and the north side, to see if there was a fresh ship, 'cos I'd been there the day before and I could recognize a fresh ship, and I'd try to estimate whether there was the chance of a day's work. With a bit of luck, you might even get two days, or half a day, or it might be nothing at all. The south side was best because there was so many wharves, Mark Brown's had the Baltic ships and the Charl boats from the Mediterranean. The Baltic ships used to discharge bacon which had to be loaded into the warehouses across the road, so you'd get up to a hundred truckers hired in the day, then it would be finished. You also had Wilson's wharf or Hays wharf, so there was always a better chance of getting a day's work on the south side, always.

But sometimes you might get unstuck. You'd go to the south side and there'd be absolutely thousands there because Bermondsey and all round there seemed to have a bigger population of casual dock workers than the north side, Wapping and Stepney. You'd have to go home again to Wapping on the north side and you'd bang into someone who'd say, 'Why didn't you come here

London was the warehouse of the world—a bill of sale for exotic cargoes.

The physical toughness and skill of dock work is exemplified by this deal porter.

this morning you'd have got a day's work here, they were short handed.' The work was seasonal as well, in the winter time, in the timber season, you'd stand a good chance of getting work in the Surrey Docks, probably a week's work there then.

London still had the greatest port in the world at that time, but when war came its trade was cut back drastically. The Luftwaffe dropped mines into the Thames estuary, and the tugs and ships working it had to be fitted out with an electric cable which repelled magnetic mines—it was called degausing. At night the estuary was closed off. The docks were hammered in the Blitz. Black Saturday on 7 September 1940, when 400 bombers raided the docks, is emblazoned on the minds of all those surviving waterside people who witnessed it.

All the timber wharves of the Surrey Docks caught fire, and Alan Herbert, the writer of comical stories and *Misleading Cases*, described the scene as 'like a lake in hell' as the lighters caught fire and the river burned. Herbert was stationed at Southend on the boat the *Water Gypsy*, and sailed into the conflagration on the tide. Molten sugar from the West Indies burned on the surface of the Thames. As in the Great Fire of 1666, the inflammability of all the liquor and coal and sugar turned the docks into a huge bonfire. Guided by the light of the flames, the bombers returned at night killing 430 people, and the raids continued for seventy-six nights. The children of dockers were evacuated at the start of the war, and gangs of dockers were recruited to load and unload supply ships around the world.

As the war turned in the Allies' favour, and the D-day landings were planned, many of the Mulberry floating harbours were built in the docks and towed down the Thames and across the Channel. Barges were given motors and turned into troop carriers. The position of the Thames, facing east towards the continent, which in peacetime was its great asset, was once again valuable. Throughout history, the position that made it vulnerable to attack from the Vikings onwards was also the trade route and the way back. Because the Thames and the east coast were so vulnerable, the distribution of goods and the shipping of troops shifted to the west coast and in particular Scotland, where gangs of London dockers were billeted to help load and unload ships.

By the end of the war, London's port was down to a quarter of its normal trade, and much of it was burned out and in ruins. About one-third of the river and dock warehousing and quays had been destroyed

As a result of the Blitz during the last war, the trade of London's port was reduced to about a quarter.

out of a total of sixteen miles of river front wharves, and seven major dock systems in which there were thirty-eight individual docks and basins. Most of the Surrey Docks, the warehouses of the West India Dock, and all of St Katherine's Eastern Dock buildings had gone or were severely damaged.

But the port was not dead. In fact, it flourished for another twenty years after the war, as £108 million was spent on it by the PLA, and great efforts were made to improve the handling of cargo. The peak year in history for the port was 1961 when it handled 60 million tonnes of goods.

Timber goes up in flames in the Surrey Docks during the Blitz.

An attempt was made to get rid of the old evil of casual labour, and a great many dockers were paid off. Increasingly, the PLA became the last employer of dockers laid off elsewhere. Between September 1967 and January 1970, thirty-two riverside wharves closed, and the number of lightermen fell from 5,000 in 1959 to 2,000 in 1969. A great deal of the port work was shifting down to Tilbury which could handle the larger ships, and when the timber went there in 1970 the Surrey Docks closed, and the deal porters, balancing springing planks of softwood on their shoulders, disappeared from the London scene.

At Tilbury they were getting the ocean passenger traffic going with proud new waiting rooms and baggage handling, when the first jet—the Comet—took to the air. Nobody foresaw how fast air travel would take off—Heathrow was just a huddle of tents at that time, and Croydon was London's main airport. Now, in the heart of the old docklands there is the new London City Airport.

A NEW FACE FOR DOCKLANDS

The docks began closing down just after the port reached its historic peak. In 1967 the East India and Regent's Canal Docks closed. A year later St Katherine's Dock—which had been given a new entrance lock from the river in 1957—and the London Docks closed. After the Surrey Docks had gone, there was a breather and some prospect of the Royals surviving. But everything was conspiring to kill the old docks off—not least the realization that the value of the land here, which had been more or less worthless marsh when the docks were built, was rising. A whole spate of dock disputes about the use of non-union labour and then about containerization of goods provided an unhappy end. The West India Docks closed in 1980, then the Millwall which had been refitted after the war with the very latest technology. Last to go were the Royal docks—Victoria, Albert and George V—in 1981.

A large part of this vast derelict area was handed over to a new body—the London Docklands Development Corporation in 1981, and its history since then has been almost as dramatic as anything in the past. To escape the work practices of Fleet Street, Times Newspapers moved to Wapping, where there were ugly scenes as print workers tried to prevent the new print works from operating. A resistance to the infiltration of City folk by the last of the remaining docklands communities is expressed in graffiti: 'Mug a Yuppie', 'Hands off our Waterfront'.

The derelict West India Docks on the Isle of Dogs in 1988 being transformed into an area of office blocks and futuristic housing. The light railway crosses the old quays; the 'Blood Alley' of the sugar quays becomes a boom town.

Few commercial uses for the riverside remain as the wharves have tumbled down. It is a selling point for estate agents offering marina-style housing, and—in a nice reversal of the general trend—lightermen are towing barges up to Canary Wharf delivering building materials for a brand new trade centre.

The overall impression is not simply of a vanished world, but in many ways of history repeating itself, for this enormous region was carved out by competing commercial interests in the nineteenth century, and a large part of the Isle of Dogs has been handed back to those very same entrepreneurial forces. It was made an 'Enterprise Zone' free of many planning and building restrictions to encourage investment. The resulting mish-mash of developments fills some with horror and others with admiration for the unplanned vigour of free enterprise. It is astonishing how fast the area has changed in just ten years or so. But for those who lived through the building of the West India Docks, the East India Docks, the Surrey Docks, the London Dock, and St Katherine's Dock in the first thirty years of the nineteenth century, the transformation must have been even more fantastic.

What should be remembered is that much of the wealth that has been generated in the past centuries through the trade of the port, the ingenuity of ship-builders, merchants, and sailors, and the sweat and skill of dockers and lightermen, has accumulated in the City. That wealth, now re-cycled through banks and dealing houses, is spilling out on to the old dockland and turning it into a very new kind of place in London, of fashionable housing and new office blocks. Dockland may have forgotten the river, but that is where its money came from.

Bill Reegan, returning to the Isle of Dogs after many years, was lost. All the landmarks, all the smells which defined the geography of the port have gone though some abandoned sugar warehouses remain:

> *I suppose I'm rather numb, I don't know where I am, I can't even sort the various quays and docks out. It's just a world of buildings. And there is no character you know, the docks as you worked in them and grew up in then they all had their character appertaining to whatever cargoes that particular quay dealt with and you sort of ... when someone said North Quay you thought of sugar, when somebody said South Quay you thought of dates or copper, which used to come over in big square plates, or tea. And so the various quays had their smells, you could smell sugar—North Quay sugar coming at you.*

The new face of dockland at Heron Quays on the Isle of Dogs: a sprit-sail barge becomes a museum piece. The rapid transformation of the whole of docklands has astonished those who knew it as a working port.

ROADS & THE RIVER

3

There was a time when a journey on the Thames could be much faster and more convenient than a trip through the crammed and narrow streets of London. In December 1667, Samuel Pepys records in his diary a journey from the City to Whitehall: 'By coach to the Temple, and then, for speed by water thence to Whitehall.' It seems astonishing today that getting out of a carriage so near to Whitehall to take a boat should make a journey quicker. But the streets of London then were regarded by all commentators as dreadful: rutted, full of water, crammed with people and horse traffic.

In Pepys's day there was only one bridge across the Thames in London itself, and that was the horribly congested Old London Bridge, narrow, dark and covered with shops and houses. Upstream there was no bridge until Kingston, and downstream no way across the water except with the ferries. By modern standards nearly all travel was extremely slow, and those who imagine that the traffic jam arrived with the motor car should read the accounts of the frustrations of Victorian commuters in the days of the horse bus.

The Thames has always been both a highway and a barrier. There is a long history of conflict between those wanting to build bridges across the Thames to improve road transport, and those opposing bridges because they make navigation of the river more difficult and hazardous. Tower Bridge is the most evocative monument to this conflict. It opens infrequently these days, but it was designed to allow through a steady stream of ships going to and from the Pool of London, and at the same time to provide a river crossing for the heavy road traffic of London's upper port. Whenever it opened for ships—which always had priority—it held up the traffic. The operation of the bridge by steam-driven machinery and hydraulic power ran very smoothly as a rule so that the interests of road and river traffic were served. But as Stan Fletcher, who was one of the operators of the great bascules in the old days before electrification recalls, there could be problems:

> This one particular vessel, the Jeannie, about two and a half thousand tonnes, was quite small but big enough to need the bridge. It would come up two possibly three times a week for the Baltic trade, bringing bacon and eggs from Denmark and Poland, and it was always a tidal boat, it came up with the tide and you were expecting him. Round the corner comes a vessel and you probably say, 'Oh, it's the Jeannie, okay, take her up.'

The grand opening of Tower Bridge in 1894. It exemplified the conflict between road and river traffic: ships had to be allowed into the Pool of London, while the demand for a river crossing had grown with the development of traffic between the north and south sides of the port.

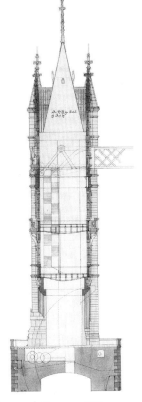

The steel frame of Tower Bridge is clad in stone to reflect its historic position next to the Tower of London. It is 'the' symbol of London and the Thames.

Now the problem is that the boat has been up here so many times, he doesn't slacken down, you've always raised the bridge and literally you've not actually finished raising the bridge before the boat's gone through ... and of course, it happened on this particular day that something went wrong. He suddenly realized the bridge wasn't going to move and he's coming closer and closer ... Eventually he went astern and, we got the bridge up and he came through and the air was blue as you can imagine ... we didn't have a radio at that time, which is just as well, because I think it would have been very personal ... but I mean, it was, it was on the megaphone, you know, what sort of people we were, what our ancestry was, things like that, and of course he unloaded his cargo and went out a couple of nights later and then he came back the second trip that week and he came steaming round the corner so I said, 'Look, it's the Jeannie', *we whacked the bridge up. Then he stopped and he came up at a slow speed and there we are, we're cocked in the air, we've got the traffic building up and the traffic was very heavy in those days, and this built up all around and of course you've got all the motorists and the lorry drivers, 'What's going on?', but you can't bring the bridge down till boat's gone through and he deliberately crept all the way through.*

Tower Bridge was the last of the great river crossings to be built in the nineteenth century, by which time the Thames had been bridged by road and rail many times above London Bridge. In London's central area, above the port, the interests of land traffic had, over two centuries, overridden those of river traffic. It had been a long and hard-fought battle.

For more than 500 years after its completion in 1209, Old London Bridge stood alone. It was a monumental edifice, supported on nineteen arches of variable span, each encased in enormous foundations or 'starlings' to protect them from the scouring of the water. The bridge provided the City with a monopoly of land traffic across the Thames, and acted as a barrier to shipping. Large ships had to stop below it. There was a small drawbridge in the middle—a forerunner of Tower Bridge which allowed passage to some vessels. But the rush of water between the arches was hazardous to all boats, and 'shooting' the bridge was a dangerous business. Except for twenty minutes or so when the tide was on the turn, the Thames rushed through the narrow arches and watermen taking their wherries through had to shoot the bridge, taking in their oars and hoping they came out the right way up on the other side.

There were many royal journeys from Windsor to Hampton Court down to Greenwich, but precious few accounts of how the various historical luminaries chose to get past London Bridge. We know that Cardinal Wolsey regularly visited Henry VIII down at Greenwich Palace and that he chose not to risk getting wet or—as happened not infrequently—drowning. He would get out of his splendid barge at 'The Crane' stairs above the bridge where his mule, decked out in crimson velvet and bronze gilt stirrups, was waiting, and ride along Thames Street preceded by attendants carrying his hat, the Great Seal and silver crosses. When his barge had shot through the bridge, he re-embarked at Billingsgate and was rowed down to Greenwich.

From the Middle Ages until the mid-eighteenth century, Old London Bridge was regarded as one of the wonders of the world. It was not just a bridge, but an integral part of London itself. Not only did it

Old London Bridge acted as a barrier across the Thames, its narrow arches holding back the flow of water and marking the up-river limit of larger ships. In this 1600 depiction, Southwark, on the south bank, is to the left.

effectively dam the river, it hummed with life. When it was being built there was the problem of raising the enormous amount of money to bring in the stone and timbers and the craftsmen. A tax on wool provided some money; King John made a grant; and the churches and many City people bequeathed land and legacies to 'God and the Bridge'. From an early date it was proposed that shops and houses should be built on it to provide funds for its upkeep in the form of rents. Exactly when the first wooden houses were put up on the stone structure of the bridge is unclear: the records for the early years of the bridge are poor.

Kentish ragstone from the Medway brought up in barges was laid on top. The designer of the stone bridge, the priest-builder Peter of Colechurch, did not live to see it completed, and the slowness and difficulties gave rise to a very uneven structure. None of the arches was the same width, and there was considerable variation between some. Those who drew it in the first centuries of its existence provide very different views, and the bridge never looks quite the same in any of them. The constant need to repair the bridge added to its unevenness, and the great starlings acting as breakwaters for the piers grew larger over the years as they were patched up.

The new bridge, only twenty feet wide and covered with houses, was a bottleneck and by the early eighteenth century the capital's earliest traffic regulations were brought in to try to ease the congestion. In 1772 an order was made appointing three wardens whose job was to keep the carts, coaches and carriages moving. Their task was:

> *To direct and take care that all Carts, Coaches and other Carriages coming out of Southwark into this City, do keep all along on the West Side of the said bridge (note: that is to the left) and all Carts, and Coaches and other Carriages, going out of this City do keep all along on the East Side of the said bridge; and that no carman be suffered to stand across the said bridge, to load or to unload; and that they shall apprehend all such who shall be refractory, or offend herein, and carry them before some of his Majesty's Justices of the peace.*

It was ordered that those crossing the bridge should have their money ready: 4d. for a cart with iron wheels, 1d. for drays with five barrels, 2d. for anything over a ton weight and 1d. for under.

The tolls on the bridge helped to pay for it. But from early on in the bridge's history the establishment of a Bridge House—in which

materials for repair were kept—provided essential funds. Rents from lands left for the upkeep of Old London Bridge went into a Bridge House Trust, which still exists.

In its early days, London Bridge was more than just a bridge: it was a gateway to London, and for that reason defended by a gatehouse at the Southwark end. Visitors or invaders from the continent would land on the south coast and march to London. An alternative route was

From 1209 until the mid-eighteenth century, Old London Bridge was the only river crossing in London. This view was painted just before the Great Fire destroyed much of the bridge.

to go by land to Gravesend and to take the 'long ferry' up to Billings-gate. Although heavy cargoes would arrive by sea, negotiating the hazardous Channel waters with the Goodwin Sands always shifting and treacherous to the south of the Thames estuary, passengers preferred to avoid it.

As the main gateway to London, the bridge had a symbolic value, and in 1305 there is the first recorded instance of the gruesome custom of displaying the heads of executed miscreants and rebels on poles in the centre of the bridge. William Wallace, a Scots patriot, had his head 'set upon a pole on London Bridge'. Until 1577 the heads were displayed on the drawbridge gate in the centre of the bridge then, when this was demolished, they were moved to the great Stone Gate at the Southwark end. The sight of these rotting faces was something of a tourist attraction until 1678 when the practice ended. It is some measure of the way in which our sensibilities have changed that during the period when severed heads adorned the bridge, it was a very fashionable place to live.

The shops on the bridge were high class, as a record of those destroyed in one of the many disastrous fires records. A blaze, started by the maid of a needle-maker who put a tub of hot coal ashes under the stairs before going to bed in 1632, wiped out forty-three businesses: haberdashers, shoemakers, grocers, mercers, a 'silke man' and several hosiers among others.

CONGESTION ON OLD LONDON BRIDGE

In the seventeenth century, the need for any other bridges over the Thames was not very acute, for so much of the life of London was concentrated into a small area in the north. Although there were rumblings of discontent in Westminster, these did not become very strident until the focus of fashionable London had begun to shift. The building of new squares by landowners and speculators in the early eighteenth century drew the well-to-do away from Old London Bridge, and its reputation as a place to live went into permanent decline. At the same time, the traffic congestion on the bridge was going from bad to worse. Thomas Pennant, in his book *Some Account of London* written in the mid-eighteenth century, has this description of the Bridge:

> *I well remember the street on London Bridge, narrow, darksome and dangerous to passengers from the multitude of*

carriages; frequent arches of strong timber crossed the street, from the tops of the houses, to keep them together, and from falling into the river. Nothing but use could preserve the rest of the inmates, who soon grew deaf to the noise of the falling waters, the clamours of the watermen, or the frequent shrieks of the drowning wretches.

While London Bridge was the only permanent crossing on the Thames in the built-up area, the watermen and the ferries provided the captial's chief form of transport, and the most convenient way for passengers to cross the river. An estimate in Stow's famous *Survey of*

The London riverside in 1732 when a great deal of transport was provided by watermen who plied for hire at stairs along the riverside. Their wherries are clustered by the stairs, while on the river there is a hay barge and the grander barge of a nobleman.

London in the sixteenth century that there were 40,000 watermen is dismissed as gross exaggeration by later historians, but it is quite clear from paintings and contemporary accounts that they were a large section of the working population. Eminent people had their own barges and their own crews; City magnates and the Lord Mayor had their splendid boats rowed by liveried oarsmen; as did royalty and senior members of the government.

A transport map of the capital would consist of the list of 'stairs' lining both banks of the river, where the watermen gathered. In the eighteenth century there were about a hundred of these. The size of their boats and the numbers they could carry were regulated. There were constant disputes between watermen and lightermen over whether each could carry passengers and cargo until the two companies—not quite guilds, but regulated organizations—were merged in 1700. The skills required were essentially the same: a knowledge of the tides on the river, and an ability to manoeuvre a boat in often difficult conditions.

But travelling by boat was not necessarily regarded as great fun—it was more a necessity. In winter there was much less traffic.

A study of how Samuel Pepys travelled about town in the seventeenth century gives some idea of how the river was used by a person with the luxury of his own barge, provided when he was secretary to the Admiralty. He often hired boats, and claimed back the expenses, though he had a waterman with his own coat of arms painted on the boat. If he was in a hurry he hired a pair of oars, otherwise he used a single sculler. In winter months he might go on the river hardly at all—in January 1665 he only hired a boat once. In July that year he made twenty-nine journeys by river, compared with sixteen trips in hackney carriages.

WHEELS AND WHERRIES

The great competition for the boatmen in Pepys's time were horse-drawn coaches which had been introduced to England by a Dutchman in 1565. One was presented to Elizabeth I who began to use it for state occasions, and coaches quickly became fashionable with the very wealthy. By 1600 private and public coaches were becoming common and causing traffic jams in the streets. The watermen made much of the nuisance of carriages in town to argue against them and to protect their own trade. In 1633, they managed to get an order of Star Chamber exhorting theatre-goers to use wherries to get home:

As to a complaint of the stoppage of the streets by the carriages by persons frequenting the playhouse of the Blackfriars, their lordships remembering that there is an easy passage by water into that playhouse without troubling the streets and that it is much more fit and reasonable that those which go thither should go by water or else on foot do order all coaches to leave as soon as they have set down and not return till the play is over nor return further than the west end of St Paul's Churchyard of Fleet Conduit, coachmen disobeying these orders to be committed to Newgate or Ludgate [prisons].

A family setting out in an ornate barge around the mid-eighteenth century.

The watermen fought fiercely against the coach, with poetic broadsides unleashed by John Taylor, the 'water-poet', who wrote in 1622:

> *Carroaches, coaches, jades and Flanders mares*
> *Doe rob us of our shares, our wares, our fares,*
> *Against the ground we stand and knocke our heeles,*
> *Whilst all our profit runs away on wheels...*

Taylor came from Gloucester, was apprenticed to a London waterman and then impressed into the navy. It was the fate of many watermen at the time and they argued strongly that if they were to disappear the navy would be short of seamen in times of war. While some recognition was given to this in the years afterwards as the watermen's trade began to decline, the progress of transport in the capital inevitably took traffic away from the river, or over it. In 1637 the first Hackney carriages were licensed. Oliver Cromwell had no time for the watermen's claims and when they petitioned him to limit the increase in coaches he raised the numbers of licensed Hackney carriages from 200 to 300.

A kind or coarse repartee was the stock in trade of watermen, and the river from quite early on appears to have given licence for rude exchanges which were less acceptable on land. A young Frenchman, César de Saussure, wrote home in 1725 from London with the enthusiasm of the tourist for things the native might find irksome:

> *You cannot see anything more delightful than this river. Above*
> *the Bridge it is covered with craft of every sort; round about*
> *London there are at least 15,000 boats for the transport of per-*
> *sons ... Nothing is more attractive than the Thames on a fine*
> *summer evening; the conversations you hear are most entertain-*
> *ing, for I must tell you that it is the custom for anyone on the*
> *water to call out whatever he pleases to other occupants of boats,*
> *even were I the King himself, and no one has the right to be*
> *shocked ... Most bargemen are very skilful in this mode of war-*
> *fare using singular and quite extraordinary terms, generally*
> *very coarse and dirty and I cannot possibly explain them to you.*

In 1725 and for a long time afterwards, the watermen at the stairs in central London, with their distinctive costumes of red or green doublets, or the arms of livery companies, the king or the Lord Mayor, were still there in large numbers. De Saussure, again, records:

> *These boats are very attractive and cleanly kept, and are light*
> *in weight, painted generally in red or green, and can hold six*

The building of bridges took away much of the work of watermen, but they were still plying for hire by the stairs next to the new London Bridge in the 1830s.

persons comfortably. On rainy days they are covered with coarse strong tents and in the summer when the sun is burning hot, with an awning of thin green or red woollen stuff ... The boatmen wear a peculiar kind of cap made of velvet or black plush, and sometimes of cloth the same colour as their waistcoats. As soon as a person approaches the stairs they run to meet him calling out lustily, 'Oars, Oars,' or 'Sculler, Sculler'. They continue this melodious music until the person points with his finger to the man he has chosen, and they at once unite in abusive language at the offending boatman.

A couple descend the stairs to hire a boat from a waterman.

Watermen probably served foot passengers pretty well, but as London and its horse traffic grew, the demands for new bridges became more earnest. The only alternative to London Bridge was the Lambeth horse ferry, the franchise for which was owned by the Archbishop of Canterbury or the Fulham Ferry upstream and really quite a long way out of London. These ferries were not greatly loved by those who used them: they were unreliable, often dangerous, and disliked by horses. Indeed, documentation records that the Lambeth ferry sank in 1663 with some of the archbishop's belongings when he was moving into Lambeth Palace, and Oliver Cromwell's horses went down with it in 1656. Nicholas Hawksmoor, the architect and student of Sir Christopher Wren wrote of the ferry in 1726: 'There is no need to say anything of the Badness and Inconveniency of Lambeth Ferry, since there is scarce anyone ignorant of it, and some have found it to their Cost.' In 1701 an order had been made to fine watermen operating the ferry 2s. 6d. if they upset the passengers as they 'do often use such immodest, obscene and lewd Expressions towards Passengers and to each other ...'

A proposal to build a bridge at Westminster to replace the horse ferry was put forward as early as 1664. This went to the king's privy council, attended by the Lord Mayor of London, the bailiff and magistrates of Westminster, the ferry 'farmers' (those who ran it) and the Company of Watermen.

Those in favour argued that it would make the trip from Westminster to Hampton Court, Whitehall and Greenwich much easier, would help trade in Westminster, and would be useful if the allegedly rebellious people of Southwark, 'a notorious district' of beer gardens, theatres and bowling alleys, got out of hand for troops to suppress them could be despatched over the new bridge.

Those against—the City and the watermen—raised a string of objections. The gist of this was that the new bridge would take trade away from Southwark, reduce the toll money on London Bridge so that it would fall into disrepair, wreck the whole of the City's economy, dam the river so that the town would flood, make trade impossible with towns up-river, throw 30,000 watermen out of work, thus depriving the navy of its chief strength in time of war, and lead to an expansion of London which would put more sewage and filth into the river than ever before.

It was a cogent argument with some justice in it, but not half as convincing as the £100,000 the City lent to the king in return for scrapping the scheme. From then on, for nearly another century, the opposition of the City and the watermen prevented any more bridges being built. Exactly the same kind of opposition was voiced when a proposal came up for a bridge at Fulham in 1671, debated this time by a House of Commons committee. A dissenting voice was heard from Mr Secretary Trevor: 'No laws can be made but will transfer one or other inconvenience somewhere, passages over rivers are generally convenient; and by the same reason you argue against this bridge, you may argue against London Bridge and the ferries.'

In the end, of course, that view had to prevail, but it was not until 1729 that London got its second bridge, at Fulham. A spur to this was the annoyance of Sir Robert Walpole at being held up on his way to the Commons because the Fulham ferryman was drinking in the Swan Tavern, leaving his boat high and dry and hearing no shouts for assistance from clients wishing to cross the river. Walpole was one of those who subscribed to the building of the wooden bridge, which was completed in only eight months.

It was characteristic of all developments in London that it was privately financed, and tolls were introduced to help to pay for it. Compensation was paid to the owners of the ferry, the Bishop of London and the Duchess of Marlborough, to the tenants of the ferry who got £8,000 and to the watermen who got £62 in perpetuity for themselves and their families. Buying out ferry and watermen's rights was to be an expensive business.

While the battle was being fought for Fulham Bridge, a renewed attempt to get one built at Westminster began with two petitions to Parliament in 1721. This time there was a good deal of backing from landowners in Kent, Sussex, Surrey and Southampton, and it was

A rather bizarre depiction of the Lambeth horse ferry from 1706. Westminster Bridge was built here in 1750, but the old horse ferry continued to run for some time afterwards.

argued that the old ferry was hopeless for passenger transport and carrying produce to Westminster. The whole of the West End was being
built up, with new squares appearing in Mayfair. The same battle
ensued with the City and the watermen: with one new opponent, the
proprietors of Fulham Bridge, who were doing well with £49 a week
in tolls and did not want competition.

Getting Westminster Bridge built proved to be a long-drawn-out
affair. But when the new Westminster Bridge was opened on Saturday
18 November 1750 with great ceremony, the monopoly of Old London Bridge and the ferrymen was gone for good. The *Whitehall*

Evening Post reported a meeting at the Bear at Bridge Foot, toasts being drunk, a salute with forty-one pieces of cannon, trumpets and kettle drums sounding, a procession over the bridge and 'God Save The King' being sung on the central arch.

Yet, in 1739, writing in *The Champion*, the novelist Henry Fielding had called Westminster Bridge then under construction 'The Bridge of Fools'. Public lotteries were all the fashion, and there were five held to raise money for the bridge. All were quite inadequate, the last being held in 1741 when the first prize was £10,000, and the lowest £10. Ironically, two of the winners of the last lottery were watermen, one from Richmond and one from Ratcliffe, who got £500. Part of the cost of building the bridge was the £25,000 paid to the watermen in compensation for loss of business. The Archbishop of Canterbury got £21,025 for loss of business on the horse ferry, which continued to run until the early nineteenth century, and is still remembered in the street in Westminster, Horseferry Road.

Parliament had to pay for the bridge in the end, and it was regarded as a very fine structure once it was opened, lit at night by oil lamps and toll-free. The City, which was the main opponent of new bridge building and the authority best able to fund bridges, had to respond. All the houses on Old London Bridge were demolished in 1762 and the bridge was widened to ease traffic congestion. At the same time the City began work on a new bridge at Blackfriars which was opened in 1768. The Bridge House Estate, formed for the financing and upkeep of Old London Bridge, provided security for a loan to build Blackfriars, along with toll charges.

Battersea Bridge, promoted by Earl Spencer and financed privately, was opened in 1776. It was not a financial success, for the receipts from tolls hardly paid for repairs, but it was thought to be a pleasing and useful ornament for London. Further upstream, at Kew, the enterprising proprietor of the ferry applied to build a bridge. This opened in 1749, a year before Westminster Bridge.

The building of bridges was no longer a contentious issue, and many more were thrown across the Thames in the nineteenth century. Vauxhall Bridge, an entirely speculative venture, was opened in 1816. The money was found with a Parliamentary loan against the income from tolls. It was the first cast iron bridge across the Thames. Waterloo Bridge was opened in 1817, designed by the great engineer John Rennie, who also worked on Southwark Bridge opened in 1819.

An engraving by Piranesi (above) of the design for the first Blackfriars Bridge in the 1760s. This was later replaced by the present Victorian bridge.

The original Westminster Bridge in 1790 from King's Arms Stairs in Lambeth (opposite). Though watermen were compensated for loss of business when the bridge was built they continued to ply for hire.

Although it was between two of the City's bridges, Southwark was promoted by a private company despite great opposition.

The City finally took the bridge over. In 1827, London's first suspension bridge was built at Hammersmith. By that time, Old London Bridge was doomed: John Rennie had begun work on a new bridge upstream in 1823, and the old bridge was finally demolished in 1831 when its replacement was opened.

It is some measure of the power of the Thames as a river and the difficulties of bridging it that none of the structures mentioned above survives. They have all been replaced at least once, and in many cases twice, because of structural failings.

The complaints that the watermen made that the bridges would make navigation of the river much more difficult turned out to be true. They had to develop new skills learning how the tides 'set' about bridge piers—although there were some compensations, as Bill Brown recalls from his days as an 'up-river' lighterman:

If you had a good tide under you, you'd take the paddle aft, all you had to do then was stand and steer the barge, it used to be lovely that did, especially when you're going through the bridges, standing there with a little dog-end in your mouth.

If it was windy, you might be lucky, someone's hat might blow off and into your barge, you'd jump down and see if it fitted you, invariably it would be a bowler hat, someone going over the bridge to London Bridge Station. The bloke would be shouting down to you, 'Where's my hat?' If it fitted you you didn't answer, if it didn't you told him where you were going, so he could pick it up if he wanted. Cor blimey, I've had some hats at high water down there.

The greatest problem was for the larger ships going up-river to power stations and gasworks. In particular the collier ships which were eventually especially designed to fit under the arches of the bridges—just. They had to go up on a rising tide but had to time it so that there was enough water to float them, but not so much they hit the bridges. Watermen acting as pilots—'bridge' or 'mud pilots' as they are called—would go on to the colliers at Cherry Garden Pier below Tower Bridge. Albert Dale was captain of one of the colliers with folding funnels known as 'flat irons':

> *The early steam-powered flatties had a whacking great big funnel, which had to be taken down to go under the bridges, it was held down by a wire, the ventilators from the engine room, the fireman had to work harder as there was no funnel or chimney to help his draft, even the galley funnel had to come down. That was the cook's job. We all used to get another half-crown for the effort.*
>
> *When we arrived at the Lower Pool we had to wait for the tide. Then we got a mud pilot, a bridge pilot, a local man with local knowledge and a lot of experience and he would take us up through the bridges to Battersea, Fulham or Wandsworth Gas. He had marks by the stones on the bridges to check the water and I remember one saying, 'How many stones can you see?' In the dark it wasn't easy. If the tide rose quicker than expected, we had to increase our speed to make sure we got underneath the bridges. One of the pilots used to have a bit of fun by Dolphin Square on the way to Fulham, he used to blow a long blast of the whistle, underneath this railway bridge, which had millions and millions of starlings roosting and the whole mob used to come out shrieking, they had a right royal time, they usually peppered us with the usual stuff. The residents of Dolphin Square used to complain especially if it was at night, we used to wake the whole neighbourhood up. But he used to do it religiously every time.*

Mud pilots Dick Waterhouse and Frank Wilson worked from Cherry Garden Pier for many years. Dick remembers:

> *We boarded the ships at Hanover buoys, the masters were always pleased to see us, we'd take over as master of the ship. We had to check for the height of the water at Battersea Power Station and the Grosvenor Road Railway Bridge to ascertain*

A 'flat-iron', the South Eastern Gas Board collier Ewell *with its funnel and mast down as it goes under the Albert Bridge in the 1930s. The building of bridges made navigation of the Thames much more difficult, and the flat-irons were designed especially to negotiate them.*

whether we were going to have enough draught to get through Westminster Bridge ... which was so low if you stood on the catwalk you could actually see the people walking on the pavement. You would think that it was going to take the wheelhouse out. As the full part of the ship entered the arch, the arch was so narrow it displaced the water to allow the ship to go underneath the bridge, and as the stern of the ship went through, if you looked back, you could see the ship rise again in the water.

Inevitably there were mishaps. Frank Wilson:

You had marks on the bridges, so you knew how much water you needed to get through the bridge. If the water was too high there was a danger of getting stuck, or taking the wheelhouse off; if the water was too low, there was a danger of running aground.

I remember one incident, I was coming down the river on a coaster called the Keystone. *There had been heavy rain and the river had built up, so we couldn't get under Teddington Foot Bridge, so the skipper decided to go under the bridge anyway. In the wheelhouse, he could see over the top of the bridge. The skipper just went down and sawed the wheelhouse off.*

Another time I was coming down from Brentford Dock, they was painting Hammersmith Bridge and there was scaffolding then on wires and poles hung across the bridge, about three feet down from the arches. I misjudged the height coming down and caught the scaffold pole right in the corner of the wheelhouse, which lifted the roof right off, all the windows fell in and it nearly frightened the life out of the helmsman at the wheel.

The bridges remain a problem for the few ships left plying the Thames above London Bridge and, of necessity, the building of bridges took work away from the watermen. But it was still possible to get a skiff or a wherry even at the end of the nineteenth century, and though sadly diminished in numbers, the watermen were still a feature of London when Henry Mayhew interviewed them for his *Life and Labour in London* in 1850. In fact, Mayhew attributed their decline not so much to the competition of road traffic and bridges as to the coming of the steamboats. Since the demolition of Old London Bridge these larger vessels could now steam from Westminster down river.

Up-river watermen with their wherries at Richmond, Surrey, about 1835.

A great day of celebration in 1880 when the tolls on bridges in central London were removed after the Metropolitan Board of Works bought them from private, profit-making businesses. Here the freeing of Wandsworth, Putney and Hammersmith Bridges of tolls is greeted with popular revelry and an old toll gate is thrown into the river.

Mayhew believed there were 1,600 watermen left in 1850, and that there were still seventy-five stairs from which they worked. One of the watermen told him:

> *… people may talk as they like about what's been the ruin of us—it's nothing but new London Bridge. When my old father heard that the old bridge was to come down, 'Bill,' says he, 'it'll be up with the watermen in no time.' If the old bridge had stood how would all these steamers have got through it all. At some tides, it was so hard to shoot London Bridge that people wouldn't trust themselves to any but watermen. Now any fool might manage. London Bridge, Sir, depend on it, has ruined us.*

The first Thames steamer, the *Margery*, which plied between the Dundee Arms, Wapping and Gravesend in 1815 had afforded the watermen much amusement, according to Mayhew. It was not a paddle-steamer, but had wheels rather like ducks' feet attached to the stern which made a terrific splashing. Its paddles often broke off and it took five and a half hours to get to Gravesend, compared with an hour and a half on the paddlesteamers. Watermen called it the 'Yankee Torpedo' after an American steamer that had blown up. Their mirth was short-lived, however, for the paddlesteamers made life difficult for them.

At first they got plenty of work rowing passengers to and from the steamers moored in the river. But the steamer companies, which increased rapidly in number in the 1840s, found it more convenient and cheaper for their passengers if they had piers built out into the river. At the same time, the wash of the steamers upset the watermen's boats, frightening those passengers who wanted to enjoy a quainter way of travelling down the river. Mayhew quotes a waterman who was plying for hire near the Tower:

> *There's very few country visitors take boats now to see sights upon the river. The swell of the steamers frightens them. Last Friday a lady and gentleman engaged me for 2s. to go to the Thames Tunnel, but a steamer passed and the lady said: 'Oh look what a surf! I don't like the venture,' and so she wouldn't go, and I sat five hours after that before I'd earned a farthing.*

Mayhew noted sadly the few watermen left above the bridge trying to get fares at Waterloo and Southwark bridges for the price of the bridge toll and below the bridge many of them rowing up to sailing ships heading to London to offer their services as pilots—a service they still perform.

Reading th

At Pulney Bridge
The Princess & the Bridge Keeper's Daughter. *First Man a*

FREE FOR EVER

Leaving Hammersmith Bridge

Throwing the Old Gate into the river

The heyday of the steampackets on the Thames engaged in the serious business of commuter traffic was brief: from 1830 to the 1850s. In 1835, it was estimated that 670,000 passengers travelled on the Gravesend steamboats, rising to over a million the following year. But the steamers had almost disappeared ten years later, despite the fact that commuting from London to Gravesend had increased three-fold. Railway lines, London to Southend on the north side of the river, and the North Kent line on the south, had taken all the traffic. The same was true up-river. Very quickly, the steamers both on the upper reaches of the Thames and down to the holiday resorts like Margate, were only taken for the fun of the trip. (There is more about them in chapter 4).

As the railways began to surround London, they created an appalling traffic problem. Everything was horse drawn on the roads until the electric tram and then the motor car appeared at the turn of the century. Because few lines crossed the river, people arriving at London Bridge or Waterloo had to contend with bottlenecks the like of which are hardly imaginable even today. One of the problems, especially on the routes into the City, was that there were only three bridges across the Thames which did not charge a toll: London Bridge, Blackfriars and Westminster. The fact that they were free attracted a disproportionate amount of traffic to them, and London Bridge was notoriously slow to cross. It would regularly take at least fifteen minutes in the rush hour.

Southwark Bridge had toll gates at either end, and was hardly used while the toll-free Blackfriars and London bridges were jammed. The City set out in 1849 to buy Southwark Bridge, but because of haggling over the price it did not own it until 1866. Even before the narrow toll gates came down traffic increased ten-fold on Southwark Bridge after it was made a free crossing.

A few years later, London's first ever overall planning authority, the Metropolitan Board of Works, set out to ease the traffic problem by buying up private bridges and making them toll free. Between 1878 and 1880 they spent £1,400,000 on the task, freeing eleven bridges, and in 1879 the Prince and Princess of Wales spent the day on Victoria's birthday, 24 May, driving across Lambeth, Vauxhall, Chelsea, the Albert and Battersea bridges to celebrate toll-free river crossings. Old bridges were re-built, and new ones constructed: the Albert suspension and Wandsworth Bridge had been built in 1873.

East of London Bridge, the Metropolitan Board of Works opened the Woolwich Free Ferry for east Londoners north and south of the river who had contributed to the freeing of old bridges and building of new ones to the west without benefit to themselves.

Finally, there was the grand scheme for a new bridge to unite the busy dockland areas downstream of London Bridge. The City with its enormous funds was given the task of financing and choosing the designer. A host of futuristic schemes were put forward, but in the end a design selecting the architecture of the Tower was chosen. It had to be a bridge that opened to allow shipping into the Port of London, and so arose the most celebrated structure in London. With great ceremony the Tower Bridge was opened in June 1894.

Remarkably, the watermen were still around on the river in those days, partly because the traffic on the bridges remained so heavy, but also to provide leisurely trips upstream. Some of them had formed their own steamboat company, which became absorbed into a merged group when railways took much of the traffic away. In 1859 they won a monopoly on the operation of most passenger boats on the river.

In the 1890 edition of *Dickens's Dictionary of the Thames* all the official rates charged by watermen are listed. For example the fare from above London Bridge to Southwark Bridge was 6d. for oars and 3d. for a sculler; from Waterloo Bridge to Swan Stairs, Chelsea, 3s. for oars and 1s. 6d. for a sculler; from Shadwell Dock Stairs to Crawley's Wharf, Greenwich the same.

In London's port the watermen hung on into this century for there was work taking crews to and from ships, mooring ships to buoys in the river, and piloting ships up-river. It was difficult to build a bridge below Tower Bridge because it would interfere with shipping—the first for nearly a century is going up now at Dartford as a complement to the Dartford tunnel carrying the heavy traffic of the M25.

TUNNELLING UNDER THE THAMES

The solution to crossings in the port was to tunnel under the river, but this presented greater engineering problems than bridge building. As early as 1798 a company was formed to build a tunnel from Tilbury to Gravesend. Ralph Dodd, a civil engineer and canal builder, put up the first scheme and managed to get enough support for an Act to permit cutting the tunnel. The Thames Archway Company managed to raise £30,000 in ordinary shares and started work on the first shaft.

The last of the good old days for London watermen, as they take passengers out to the Margate steam yacht (opposite). Within a few years, the steamers had taken much of their trade away, and by churning up the river made rowing hazardous. This painting by Robert Havell is from the 1820s.

Below London Bridge where there was a great deal of shipping, tunnelling was the answer to river crossings—but it took a great deal of perseverence and ingenuity to overcome the engineering difficulties. The Brunel enterprise is satirized by the cartoonist Robert Cruikshank (below).

But the technical problems were never overcome, they could not pump water out fast enough and in October 1802 the engine house caught fire. It ended when the shaft had reached eighty-five feet.

At the same time, a new proposal was put forward by a Cornish mining engineer, Robert Vaize, nicknamed 'the Mole'. This was much more practicable: a tunnel between Limehouse and Rotherhithe which would be passable for 'Horses and Cattle, without carriages, and Foot Passengers'. Vaize, later joined by a former wrestler and weight-lifter Richard Trevithick, managed to get a fair way under the Thames using traditional mining techniques, but the tunnel caved in, nearly drowning Trevithick, and this project too was abandoned.

The answer to the problem of tunnelling under the Thames came in the most extraordinary way. While down at Chatham Dockyard to supervise some work, Marc Isambard Brunel, father of the more famous railway builder, became intrigued by the behaviour of a wood-boring mollusc. The elder Brunel always carried a magnifying glass and he was able to see how this deadly mollusc, whose head had sunk more ships than any hostile armada, was able to cut holes so efficiently. Two sharp shells sliced into the timber, and the wood was then chewed up, digested and finally exuded at the back to line the mollusc's tunnel.

This observation led directly to Brunel's patenting his 'great shield', an iron cylinder forced through the ground, with men behind bricking up the tunnel as they went. His first attempt to make use of it was with the Thames Tunnel Company formed in 1824. This tunnel was finished, but it took more than eighteen years to complete and was beset with many problems: the Press dubbed it 'The Great Bore'. It was completed by the younger Brunel, who got his knighthood after Queen Victoria visited the tunnel, arriving in the state barge.

As a tourist attraction the tunnel was a great success, but it was never opened to horse traffic: 'grand fancy fairs' were held in it, with weight-lifting, glass blowing and other stalls. However, by 1855, unable to pay a dividend, it went downhill socially and became a hang-out for prostitutes. In 1862 it was sold to the East London Railway Company, and was used for trains from 1870. It is now part of the underground network, connecting Wapping and Rotherhithe.

Many tunnels to carry road traffic, railways and the underground under the river have been built since the technological problems were solved, though they are still considerable.

This is the great tunnelling invention of the elder Brunel—the 'shield'. He was inspired in his design by the activities of a wood-boring mollusc he watched at work on ships' timbers in Chatham dockyard.

A nice depiction of the Brunel tunnel (below) *in relation to the river: shipping is not impeded.*

All the tunnelling and bridging of the river, then the rise of the private car, finally put an end to the Thames as a useful highway for people going to and from work. Even the steamers which had put out of work many watermen were a failure. The last attempt to provide a regular commuter service on any scale was made by the London County Council in 1905 with its own fleet of steamers running between Putney and Gravesend. It was abandoned after three years. The pattern of building in London and the journey to work had not followed the Thames for a long time, and the river had been by-passed. A river bus service does run from Westminster Pier, but it has no significance in the workings of public transport in London.

However, if people were reluctant to commute by river, they did enjoy the Thames much more as a playground, whether they were steaming to Southend or punting up at Oxford.

For a short while the Thames Tunnel was a fashionable resort, but it soon fell into disrepute.

CRUISING DOWN THE RIVER

From the time in the early nineteenth century that rowing and regattas became popular amusements, and paddlesteamers and chugging up-river steam launches carried trippers and holiday makers, there was a conflict on the Thames between the pleasure seekers and the watermen engaged in the serious business of carrying cargoes. The most recent and tragic episode in this long-running saga was the sinking of the *Marchioness* in August 1989. A large freighter, the *Bowbell*, smashed into the pleasure boat after dark, and more than fifty party-goers were drowned. That night is still a vivid and ghastly memory, not only for the survivors and the families of those who died, but for all who imagined the river to be a safe place for leisure and enjoyment.

There was a much greater catastrophe on 3 September 1878 at Galleon's Reach, eleven miles below London Bridge. This was the era in which paddlesteamers had become very popular with day-trippers going to Gravesend, Sheerness, Southend-on-Sea and Margate. The *Princess Alice* set off from Swan Pier by London Bridge on a fine day, steered through the busy port and steamed down to Sheerness. On the return journey, she called at Gravesend and then moved out into the river to return to London Bridge. The band on the main deck played: 'We don't want to fight, but by jingo, if we do'; some women at the other end of the ship sang hymns; there was a fight between a man and his wife; and children scampered all around the paddlesteamer as the evening light faded.

Many survivors described to an inquiry what happened next. They sensed something was wrong. The *Princess Alice* seemed to stop, waiting, then they saw the lights of a much larger steamer coming towards them. It towered over them and there was a terrible crunch. A collier, the *Bywell Castle*, had smashed into them and within moments the river was full of screaming and drowning trippers: 640 died. This was the worst disaster in British inland waters in history. For a long time afterwards, bodies were washed up on the tides. The *Princess Alice* was a wreck; the *Bywell Castle* continued to carry coal and other goods until she disappeared somewhere in the Bay of Biscay in 1883 with a cargo of cotton seed she was carrying from Alexandria to Hull.

The Thames has been enjoyed as a playground throughout history, and there have long been conflicts between those rowing or cruising for fun and those working on the river. Before the early years of the

The pageantry on Lord Mayor's Day 1789, when the Thames was still the chief highway in London.

The worst disaster in British inland waters was the collision between the Princess Alice *steamer and the* Bywell Castle, *a collier ship, with a death toll of 640. From Victorian times there were many conflicts between pleasure seekers and the commercial traffic of the river.*

nineteenth century it seems the conflict was much less, for celebrations on the river were much more communal events, pageants in which royalty and their attendant watermen put on splendid public displays. These pageants lasted until the mid-nineteenth century when they began to disappear, and the sport of rowing and the age of regattas took over the river.

To a large extent, the way the river has been exploited for fun has been influenced by the rival attractions on land, and the manner in which new forms of transport—coaches, railways and later motor-cars—affected river traffic. In the Victorian period, the upper reaches of the Thames became the playground of the well-to-do, while the tidal river remained a busy working waterway through which the Southend or Margate steamers had to navigate to give poorer Londoners their first taste of a real holiday.

The survival of Old London Bridge until the age of the steamer made possible a form of merry making on the Thames which has since disappeared. Because the bridge held back the flow of water in severe winters the river would freeze. Ice formed first along the shores, and gradually extended until the Thames was frozen solid above the bridge, and on some occasions below it. When this happened, informal 'frost fairs' would be held. These were infrequent events, in 1564–65, 1683–84, 1715–16, 1739–40 and 1813–14, for the frost had to last for weeks before the ice was solid enough to carry the weight of the stalls, carriages and bear-baiting crowds that gathered on it. The last of these fairs—and one of the grandest—took place in the winter of 1813–14, when a great mall, nicknamed City Road, was established on the ice. Once Old London Bridge was demolished, the freer flow of the tides prevented freeze-ups, though in places the Thames iced over in the 1890s.

One of the most celebrated frost fairs was held in the winter of 1683–84. The Thames was frozen over two days before Christmas, and on 1 January streets of tent-like booths appeared on the ice, forming an avenue which was called Temple Street—it ran from what was Temple Stairs. A bull ring was set up near London Bridge, and horse-drawn coaches were able to cross the ice. Watermen in desperation hitched their boats to horses to compete with the carriages. A printing press was an attraction, as the diarist John Evelyn noted:

> *The people and ladies took a fancy to have their names printed, and the day and year set down when printed on the Thames: this humour took so universally, that it is estimated the print gained £5 a day, for printing a line only, at sixpence a name, besides that he got by ballads etc.*

A royal party enjoyed this novelty when Charles II had his name, and that of his brother James, Duke of York, Queen Catherine, Infanta of Portugal, and others printed on the ice. Oxen were roasted, there were coach races and puppet plays and a good deal of drinking so that Evelyn called it a 'bacchanalian triumph'.

In 1739 the frost fair began on Christmas Day and continued until the middle of February, but with a peculiar and amusing interlude in January. On 21st, there was a partial thaw, and those living on the bridge woke up to a strange sight. The *Universal Spectator* reported:

> *… the inhabitants of the west prospect of the Bridge were presented with a very odd scene, for on the opening of their windows there appeared underneath on the river a parcel of booths, shops and huts of different forms, but without any inhabitants. Here stood a booth with trinkets, here a hut with a Dram of*

Frost fairs were a spectacular, though infrequent, feature of life while Old London Bridge survived. It was such a barrier to the flow of water that the Thames would freeze solid and support stalls, carriages and all kinds of sporting events. An ox is being roasted by Whitehall in this woodcut of the 1683–84 fair when royalty ate meat cooked on the ice.

The last of London's Thames frost fairs in 1813–14. By 1830, Old London Bridge had gone, and though the Thames sometimes froze, it never again supported a full-blown fair.

Old Gold, in another place a skittle frame and pins, and in a fourth 'The Noble Art and Mystery of Printing'.

The ice had broken up and the stalls were floating around below the bridge. Nobody was drowned, for the thaw occurred at night, and most of the valuables were recovered. Then the ice froze again, welding a jumble of stalls together in a heap.

These great freeze-ups were in fact times of terrible hardship for Londoners—not least for the watermen and others who could not work. But it is striking that the jollity involved all sections of society.

The river was in a sense free of the social class distinctions which prevailed on land, and represented a kind of liberty through the centuries. As the young French visitor, César de Saussure, had remarked in 1725, nobody had the right to be shocked on the river, not even the king himself, by what happened there or what was said. As with the frost fairs, any unusual conditions on the river prompted some kind of revelry. During a drought in 1884, the channel between Eel Pie Island and the Middlesex bank dried out and a party of people set up tables and chairs and had dinner there with champagne. At the same time the only recorded cricket match on the Thames was played.

Of the many bizarre events the river has stimulated, three stand out. The water-poet, John Taylor, attempted in the seventeenth century to sail a boat made of brown paper, a trip which ended not long after it began. In 1818, a clown from the Coburgh Theatre set off for a bet in a vessel like a wash-tub from Southwark Bridge to Cumberland Gardens. Out of the tub stuck a pole to which were tethered four geese. It is reported that the birds towed the clown quite happily at times, but they sometimes became restive. The clown, a Mr Usher, won his bet, but could find no takers to wager on a return trip. This event was followed by a large crowd, as was the race in June 1880 between a man and a dog from London Bridge to Woolwich. The dog, called 'Now Then', won easily—the man gave up at Limehouse when the dog was half a mile in the lead.

For the most part, however, the great events on the river until the late Victorian era were the Royal and City pageants. Though kings and queens were regularly carried in the royal barges through the centre of London, by far the greatest shows on water were those staged by the City Corporation. Since the thirteenth century the Mayor of London had annually presented himself for his oath of office at the Law Courts. This became a procession of mayor and aldermen to Westminster.

It was in 1422 that what became known as the Lord Mayor's Show first went by water. At first watermen's barges were hired by the livery companies, but in time they built their own magnificent vessels and the whole procession became a pageant in the sixteenth century, acted out partly on the Thames and partly in the processions to Guildhall through the streets of London.

The first of the elaborate barges was built for Sir John Norman, a draper, in 1454. The watermen rowed with silver oars. As the processions became more elaborate, there were disputes about precedence, especially between the Merchant Taylors and the Skinners. This led to an undignified race with one trying to get ahead of the other, and in 1483 the rivalry ended in a pitched battle on the river. From then on the two companies took it in turn to lead and were instructed to lash their barges together for a toast and declaration of friendship.

Huge crowds gather at a frost fair on the Thames in a seventeenth-century painting by Abraham Hondius.

The ceremonial barge of the Stationers' Company used while the Lord Mayor's Show was held on the river until the mid-nineteenth century.

In the seventeenth century the Lord Mayor's Show involved dramas or pageants written by leading playwrights, and included astonishing floats depicting a variety of themes, usually reflecting the trade of the Lord Mayor Elect. In 1616, for example, the pageant for the new mayor, who was a fishmonger, included a 'lemon tree rich in flowers and fruit with a pelican's nest and the five senses at its foot'. In another year, five islands were created on the river 'artfully garnished with all manner of Indian fruit trees, drugges, spiceries and the like, the middle island having a faire castle especially beautified'.

The dramas evolved from religious plays, and were usually performed not on the river but in St Paul's churchyard on the return from Westminster. It was the custom for the procession to start from Guildhall, then to go through the narrow streets to the Tower where the barges were waiting, the bargemaster in splendid uniform. From here eight oarsmen, one steering, rowed the barge up to Westminster, with musicians playing and cannon firing salutes from the shore. On the return journey, the companies got out at Blackfriars and returned to Guildhall via St Paul's churchyard.

In the early 1700s the first coaches were built for the street procession, allegedly because Sir Gilbert Heathcote riding on horseback in 1711 had been unseated by a 'drunken flower girl'. In 1756 the gilded coach which survives today was used for the first time.

The Lord Mayor's barge in 1808. Pageantry was a feature of the Thames in London for centuries until it began to shift to the land in the late Victorian period.

The river processions lasted until 1856, by which time the Thames was becoming crowded with steamships and horribly polluted. It was a long time after the introduction of the gilded coach that it took over completely from the barge, and that the Lord Mayor's Show finally took place only on the streets of London, but the use of the coach was a turning point for pageantry on the river.

Some of the livery companies' barges, which were in a bad state of repair, were bought in the mid-nineteenth century by the universities of Oxford and Cambridge to use as boat-houses in which they could change before races. Rowing, as we will see, had not long before become fashionable. Cambridge, it seems, never took delivery of its livery company barges for they sank off the east coast on their sea journey to the university.

Royal pageantry on the river lasted a little longer than the City's, though it never had anything of the ornate splendour of the Lord Mayor's Show. The last outing of Queen Mary's shallop, the state barge built in 1689 by William III, was in 1919 for a peace pageant on the Thames. In its prodigiously long life it had been used on many ceremonial occasions. The queen's bargemasters did not disappear with the barge: there are still twenty-three royal watermen who attend royal events on the river, and ride on the royal coach at the state opening of Parliament. The amphibious waterman is a wonderful example

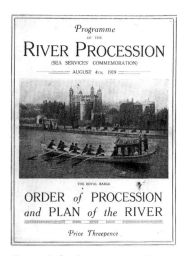

One of the last outings for the royal barge rowed by watermen was for this peace pageant to commemorate the end of the Great War.

A splendid portrait of Queen Victoria's bargemaster painted in 1843 by W. H. Noble. Today, there are still royal bargemen who attend the queen whenever she travels on the river, and take part in royal ceremonial.

A colourful evocation of Henley Royal Regatta by J. J. J. Tissot (opposite).

of professional tenacity in the face of changing fashion. It is the job of the queen's bargemaster to deliver the crown to Westminster on the state opening of Parliament. There are still some duties on the river, as Ted Hunt, recently retired as royal bargemaster, recalls:

> *Nowadays whichever vessel the queen uses is deemed to be the royal barge. When the royal party arrives you salute and stand by to offer a hand; at the embarkation end this is rarely necessary, for the river is normally closed to traffic, and there's no swell. When it is time to go it's easy for you to make your way for'ard for the gunwale is clear, and of course you're followed by your inside gunwale men and you're all in position.*
>
> *Have them all spaced between the windows on* Royal Nore, *because there's a cabin down below and windows are just above the deck. And you never know that one of them might have a ladder in his stocking; you see if they're standing between windows then people don't have to look out at a pair of spindly legs dressed in red stockings, cutting the window in half. Warn your men about hats; we nearly lost one on the day of the Thames Barrier opening.*
>
> *At your destination you should be the first man ashore, or close behind your inside gunwale man. Play it by ear. Depending on how you come round, it may be the right thing for them to nip ashore so as to make way for you.*
>
> *As she comes round,* Royal Nore *makes her own swell, which follows her. Now Maurice Line knows this and will go very very slowly up to the pier so that by the time he gets alongside and the queen steps ashore, most of the swell is gone.*

The last outing of the royal barge on the upper Thames was to carry George V and Queen Mary at Henley Royal Regatta. Just as the livery companies handed over their barges to the university rowers, so the last of the royal barges had its swansong at a rowing regatta, which by early this century had become a popular form of entertainment.

The earliest regattas were staged in the late eighteenth century. One of the first was at Ranelagh Gardens, the pleasure grounds beside the river at Chelsea, which were created around the former home of Lord Ranelagh as a rival attraction to Vauxhall Gardens, a little up-river on the opposite bank.

Whereas Vauxhall was chiefly an outdoor pleasure ground, lit with hundreds of spirit lamps, most of the stylish parade at Ranelagh was in

the Rotunda, a large circular building where the trendsetters drank tea and walked in a circle, chatting to each other. Both Vauxhall Gardens and Ranelagh Gardens were accessible by the river and provided the watermen with a good trade. Ranelagh did not last quite as long as Vauxhall, but it does appear to have had a regatta in 1775 which prompted the description: 'The ballast the city barges were used to take in was on this occasion filled with the finest ballast in the world—about 100 elegant ladies; and it is thought that the procession was seen by at least 200,000 people.'

As the tideway of the Thames became busier with shipping and, after the 1820s much more liable to serious pollution, fashion and fun tended to move up-river. Henley—the very name sounds plummy, leisured, a world away from the sweat and spice of dockland—epitomized the higher reaches of the Thames far from the pull of the tides, from industry or effort. The river here was once as much a working waterway as the stretch from Wapping to Limehouse Pier. All the charming locks and chortling weirs are industrial relics from an age of great improvements in river navigation, when barges hauled by teams of men or horses, and later steamtugs, carried coal, stone, grain, timber, slate, nearly everything between London and towns as far as Oxford on the river and beyond on the canals. The towpaths were an innovation in their day for they made the towing of barges much easier. Some of the ferries were there to carry a horse from one bank to another when the towpath switched sides.

Yet we associate places like Boulter's Lock not with sailing barges but with high society. This change of image came in the late Victorian period, around the 1880s, when the railways had begun both to kill the commercial traffic of the upper Thames and to carry out from London a new trade, the provision of pleasure for fashionable society. Watermen's boats were taken over for jolly pranks and races, converted fishermen's punts drifted around aimlessly with their catch of parasoled ladies, and barges were in turn converted to carry cargoes of cultured people living a life of ease and the hordes of the new middle classes adopting the 'paraphernalia of gentility'.

In the 1780s there is mention of barges converted into 'country

The upper Thames became a playground for fashionable Victorians, sweeping aside the commercial traffic which had been reduced by competition from the railways. Here a houseboat, complete with maids, queues at Molesey Lock in the 1890s.

houses', but the heyday of the houseboat was after the 1850s. In *The Book of the Thames*, written in 1859, Mr and Mrs C. S. Hall provide this description:

> *The interior is a spacious room; while the 'deck' affords opportunities for viewing the scenery and enjoying the pleasant breezes of the river—being furnished with benches for the convenience of such as prefer the open air ... These boats are leisurely towed up and down the river by horses and are, in fact, large and broad barges, within which the 'house' is constructed, with its windows and gaily painted or gilded panels.*

In the mid-nineteenth century, when there was still a very considerable amount of commercial traffic on the upper reaches of the Thames, the transitional period from working river to playground gave rise to some fierce social conflicts. For the drifting romantic, dangling one hand in the water, the sight of a bargee was most disturbing—they might be vulgar and inconsiderate. As the fashion for rowing and regattas spread, there were clashes over whose river this really was.

In Ascot week, Boulter's Lock was jammed with steam launches and punts as the fashionable took to the river in 1906.

Centuries of law had been in favour of the watermen against all kinds of obstructions put up by millers and fishermen because valuable goods were needed for the towns. However, once the railways had undermined the importance of the Thames for transport, the regatta people fought for the right to hold up the river for their own amusement if they wanted to.

A remarkable instance of conflict flaring up between a waterman and some rowers has been unearthed by Mary Prior in her book on Oxford fishermen, *Fisher Row*. It was reported in *Jackson's Oxford Journal* on 21 May 1884 and occurred on the boat race course near Folly Bridge. In evidence the boatman said:

> On the 12th May, between seven and eight o'clock in the evening, I was with my boat near Folly Bridge, Oxford. I had been waiting there for about an hour for the race to finish. The racing had been over about twenty minutes, and the gentlemen had got out of their boats. I started my horse over the bridge. It is a towing path bridge, and no people had any business there by rights, except those belonging to the water. It is a way that people go down the river side. I had got two or three yards before I was first stopped ... I did not by myself ... knock anyone, except it might be when they started knocking it (the horse) about. I did not strike anyone from first to last. I was stopped and they rushed in upon me. Cook used a punt-pole, he punched me on the breast with it several times; he was in a punt; the path was crowded then. A gentleman struck me with an umbrella several times ... he struck at the horse and he tried to poke me in the face ... I was covered with blood ... I think my ribs were bad from their trying to push me over the rails ...

The assailants were fined, but as Mary Prior points out the waterman's victory was short-lived: the river authority, the Thames Conservancy, solved the problem by reversing the established principles and passed a by-law in 1894 giving precedence to regattas.

From the early 1800s, when rowing as a sport began to become popular at Oxford and Cambridge and at Eton, its development provides a wonderful case study in the way a professional skill is usurped by 'amateurs', is provided with a rule book, then evolves its own kind of equipment and begins to demand a precedence for fruitless ability over useful effort. It was steeped in snobbery, and, though the amateur rule excluded them from gentlemen's regattas, the watermen were

A narrow boat on the Thames at Wallingford. Commercial river traffic had only a brief heyday on the Thames before railways and roads undermined it.

Abel Beesley, a university waterman, photographed around 1910 by Henry Taunt. When rowing began as a sport the 'amateur' rule excluded working watermen.

glad to find new employment providing for the needs of oarsmen. When amateur rowing began, the upper Thames was really near to its heyday as a highway for goods and passengers travelling up and down from London. By today's standards the pace was incredibly slow, for though the river was technically navigable it was full of obstacles. There were shallows, weirs and mills all the way along and a long-running conflict between those fishing it with wicker traps or harnessing its power to turn mill wheels which fulled (beat) wool, made paper, and provided power for breweries and tanneries.

To some extent the interest of mill owners and bargemen were the same. Both needed to control the flow of water: the miller to provide a consistent source of power; the bargees and watermen to provide enough depth in the river to float a barge. There were weirs all the way up the river, created mostly by millers and fishermen who dammed the water. In these weirs there were openings so that water could be released which would send a flood downstream, temporarily deepening the shallows. These 'flash locks' enabled the bargees to get up and down the river, but they had to wait for and pay for a 'flash'. Sometimes they were held up for weeks, or even months, haggling with the mill owner, who preferred to wait until there was a queue of boats which could be let through in one go. The London waterman and poet John Taylor made a number of trips upstream from the Pool of London and in his plodding verse described some of the hazards:

> Then Marlow Lock is worse, I must confess
> The water is so pinched with shallowness,
> Beneath which is a weare should be defaced
> And Cottrells weare of Cookham be displaced.
> A weare to noe Holdernesse belong
> Which doth the river most injurious wrong
> Near which a spring runs from the chalkie hills,
> Which not long ago did turn two mills,
> A stop against Taplow doth much spread
> Next Boulter's Lock (a mile from Maidenhead).

At the time the familiar 'pound lock' had only just been introduced to England, and the first appeared on the Thames in the 1620s. They solved the problem of bargemen waiting for a 'flash' from the miller for the barges were channelled off to one side of the river. A great effort to improve the Thames and other rivers in England was made in the seventeenth century, but the real change came in the eighteenth century, stimulated in part by competition from canals—which often took traffic away from sections of rivers—and the stage coaches. For the most part improvements were paid for by the tolls charged at locks, and Thames commissioners were appointed to make navigation of the river easier. In the late eighteenth century and early nineteenth century the river traffic between Henley and London was important, with hay, cheeses, building stone and barley going downstream, and coal coming upstream to power industries.

By the standards of the day, the river was busy when the first amateur rowers began to take an interest in racing, but these were not the first rowing competitions on the Thames. The oldest surviving regular contest, which claims to be the longest-running sporting event in the world, is the oddly named Doggett's Coat and Badge Race.

Thomas Doggett was an actor who lived in Chelsea in the early eighteenth century and performed at Drury Lane. He was accustomed to hire a wherry to take him home. The story of his founding a race for newly qualified watermen is taken up by the account in the *History*

Three men and their boat in 1873—they are having to haul it overland in order to pass a weir.

of the Watermen's Company by Henry Humpherus:

> *Mr Doggett being at one of the Stairs, wished to hire a water-*
> *man to row him up the river home, but it being a bad night and*
> *against tide, the men demurred doing so—a young waterman at*
> *length offered his services, and having accomplished the journey,*
> *Mr Doggett found on enquiry that he had only just got his free-*
> *dom of the company [finished his apprenticeship] and was very*
> *deserving of support, he therefore well rewarded him for his*
> *trouble and established this match; it being the means also of*
> *commemorating the accession of the House of Hanover to the*
> *Throne of England.*

The longest-running rowing
race on the Thames,
Doggett's Coat and Badge,
around 1820 (above).
There was heavy gambling
on this competition for
newly qualified watermen.

The race was first rowed in 1715, the winner getting prize money, an
orange coat and a badge emblazoned with the White Horse of
Hanover. It was a tough race for rugged professionals—the course
from the Swan at London Bridge to the Swan at Chelsea, rowed
against the tide in a wherry, much bulkier than today's rowing boats.
(Nowadays it is rowed with the tide in light racing craft.)

There were other rowing competitions for watermen in the eighteenth century, some of them to encourage the profession
which provided the navy with so many of its recruits in time of war. One
record in Humpherus is a race for watermen—seven boats each with
a pair of oars—from Whitehall to Putney for a prize of a silver cup
worth twenty-five guineas. It was rowed in May and started at seven in
the evening:

> *A great number of the nobility and gentry appeared in barges*
> *elegantly decorated with pendants, streamers, etc., and rowed*
> *by watermen in handsome uniforms; their Royal Highnesses and*
> *plete band of musicians, were rowed in a barge ahead of the*
> *wager men ...*

In this and other such races there was no compunction about paying
the winner. Another race recorded by Humpherus was one promoted
by West End clubs in the eighteenth century for twelve boats, each
with two young watermen, to row from Westminster Bridge, round a
boat moored by London Bridge and back again, for a first prize of ten
guineas. Tickets were limited to 1,300 and were available only to
members of the following clubs: Boodle's, White's, Stapleton's,
Almack's, Savoir-vivre or Goosetree's. The limitation was to enable
the spectators to be carried on the barges of the London livery companies. A supper was held at the famous resort, Ranelagh Gardens.

Though watermen were the
experts on the river, and
had had their own races for
centuries, those who worked
on the river could not row
at Henley or other amateur
regattas. This is W. Lyon's
boat-builders' yard in 1831
(opposite).

Doggett's is the one race that survives into the modern era. In the 1950s it became an amateur race because there were few watermen left and they no longer wanted to compete as professionals. Non-watermen were allowed to compete and the 'amateur' rule in rowing changed.

All the early records of rowing races on the Thames appear to be within London rather than upstream. Those which developed upstream and gave rise to the Victorian fashion for regattas had quite a different purpose and ethos.

In his book, *Oxford Rowing*, written in 1900, R. E. Sherwood attempts to put together the rather hazy history of how the sport began. He is concerned essentially with upper-class competitions, the sort of thing the right people accept as being a rowing race, a match of skill between men of the leisured class. He imagines groups on boating trips on the river deciding to race between one lock and another, and this developing into an organized ritual. In the early 1800s, all the boats were hired from watermen who were the experts that enthusiasts looked to for advice. There were casual races betwen university teams and sometimes watermen would be involved, but not for long. This was thought to be unfair, and chaps would run along the towpath shouting, 'No hired watermen.' A source of conflict was the watermen's delight in 'fouling' the opponents' boat by ramming it, or knocking away oars. The definition of an amateur came to mean not a person who rowed for the fun of it, without prize money, but someone who did not in their everyday job row for a living.

The first Oxford and Cambridge boat race was rowed at Henley in 1829. It attracted a crowd of 20,000 to the town—still a small place on the Thames which Daniel Defoe had described dismissively in the 1720s in his *A Tour Through The Whole Island Of Great Britain*:

> *There are two other towns on the Thames viz Henley and Maidenhead which have little or nothing remarkable in them; but that they have great business also, by the trade for malt and meal and timber for London, which they ship, or load, on their great barges for London, as the other towns do.*

Henley Regatta began not as a serious rowing event but as a tourist attraction promoted by the town itself. At a public meeting in the town hall on 26 March 1839 the following resolution was passed:

> *That from the lively interest which has been manifested at the various boat races which have taken place on the Henley Reach during the last few years, and the great influx of visitors on such*

occasions, this meeting is of the opinion that the establishing of an annual regatta, under judicial and respectable management, would not only be productive of the most beneficial results to the town of Henley, but from its peculiar attractions would also be a source of amusement and gratification to the neighbourhood, and to the public in general.

The recent races referred to were those rowed intermittently from 1829 and included those between Oxford and Cambridge teams. The promoters of the regatta were not themselves rowing people, and they can have had little idea how phenomenally successful their regatta would become. Until the railway arrived, and the regatta developed as part of the London season, it was a modest occasion with very little mention in the press, except for the results.

At the time the regatta was founded there were no accepted rules for racing—who could compete and on what terms. Oxford and Cambridge colleges had begun to devise some rules for their odd Bumping Races. Otherwise, in races for prize money or sweepstakes, the competitors simply agreed terms. From the start, when it was a small affair, the regatta reflected its upper-class origins. Here the leisured classes of early Victorian England were rowing for fun, whereas watermen had previously rowed for money, often watched by royalty and gentry, their employers. Just three rules were laid down at first in May 1839 for the first Grand Challenge Cup. The first defined who could take part:

That any Crew composed of Members of a College of either the Universities of Oxford, Cambridge or London, the Schools of Eton or Westminster, the Officers of the two Brigades of Household troops, or of members of a Club established at least one year previous to the time of entering, be considered eligible.

The clubs were to be amateur, but defining exactly what that meant was a problem.

By the 1870s, the regatta was well enough known to attract its first foreign entrant from New York. Then, in 1878, when the regatta was becoming as much a social event as a rowing competition, there was an invasion from North America. This included a crew of French Canadian lumberjacks who entered for the Stewards' Cup and alarmed officials by issuing battle cries as they rowed up Henley Reach. Henley stewards were troubled by the vulgar intrusion, and by the fact that some American crews were paid to compete, so they defined 'amateur'.

A spectacular vista of the river at Henley in the late nineteenth century when it was so crowded that the rowing races were impeded and you could cross the Thames stepping from one boat to the next.

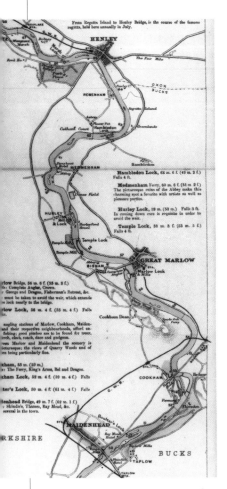

A Victorian oarsman and angler's map of the Thames between Henley and Maidenhead around the time Jerome K. Jerome's novel Three Men in a Boat *captured the appeal of the Thames for the middle classes.*

No person was to be considered eligible as an oarsman or sculler or coxswain if they had ever competed for a stake or for money (foreign crews exempt); had ever competed against a professional for a prize; had ever taught, pursued or assisted in the practice of athletic exercises of any kind as a means of gaining a livelihood; had been employed in or about boats for money or wages; who was or had been by trade or employment for wages a mechanic, artisan or labourer. Foreign crews had to make declarations that they were eligible after perusing the rules.

Henley's rules applied only at Henley—they had no wider implications. Those excluded by them had begun in the nineteenth century to set up their own tradesmen's rowing clubs and to found their own competitions and regattas. However, the Henley definition of an amateur was taken over by the Metropolitan Rowing Association, founded in 1879, which became in 1882 the Amateur Rowing Association (ARA). It not only narrowed Henley's definition of 'amateur' by excluding anyone 'engaged in a menial duty', but also laid down general rules for all regattas. This meant in effect that a large section of the population which liked to row for fun was excluded from amateur regattas because of the job they did.

A rival association naturally sprang up. The National Amateur Rowing Association (NARA) was founded in 1890 to provide an organization and regatta rules for those excluded by the definition of 'amateur' by the ARA. The new NARA classed as amateur anybody who did not row for prize money, or work professionally on boats—with special dispensation for Royal Naval officers and those of the Merchant Navy. Thus two quite different amateur rowing organizations effectively divided enthusiasts on social class lines, for both associations forbade their members to compete with each other.

The results of these exclusions were often absurd and very embarrassing for the sport. In 1919, a crew of servicemen were not allowed to row in a peace regatta held to celebrate the end of the Great War—they were members of the NARA not the ARA and in the wrangling over the definition of amateur they were excluded from Henley, much to the displeasure of George V. In 1920, the American J. B. Kelly, father of the film star Grace Kelly, was not allowed to row at Henley, even though he had won the Olympic sculls and was, under international rules, an amateur.

In 1936, Henley refused to allow the Australian Olympic crew to compete because they were policemen, and therefore 'manual

The picture of a busy Hammersmith Bridge on Boat Race Day by Walter Greaves looks more fanciful than it really is: such was the popularity of the 'Battle of the Blues' that every available vantage point was taken.

workers', but by the 1950s past absurdities were mostly eliminated. Meanwhile, the rowing at Henley had become a secondary event for most people. In 1851 it had been made the Royal Regatta when Prince Albert became its patron, and by the 1880s was an established part of the London season. *Dickens's Dictionary of the Thames* (1890 edition) remarks:

> *This, the most important gathering of amateur oarsmen in England, takes place usually about the beginning of July, and almost ranks with Ascot among the favourite fashionable meetings of the season ... One of the favourite points of view was, for many years, the* Red Lion *lawn where, at the conclusion of*

the regatta, the prizes are distributed, but by far the most popular resort is the river itself. Indeed, of late years, this has become so much the case, and the river is so inconveniently crowded with steam launches, houseboats, skiffs, gigs, punts, dinghies, canoes and every other conceivable and inconceivable variety of craft, that the racing boats have sometimes the greatest difficulty in threading a way through the crowd.

It became a perennial joke in *Punch* and other publications that few people at Henley were interested in the rowing. The regattas lasted three days in the 1830s, and it became fashionable to have lavishly furnished houseboats towed up to the course where they could command the best view of the races and socialize. The great demand for boats of all kinds brought in the watermen, who found a new trade as the railway took away their former livelihood.

In the 1853 edition of *Jackson's Oxford Journal*, the Revd Vaughan Thomas wrote a series of letters which chronicled the commercial decline of the river:

Trade, prosperous trade, may be said to have taken flight from the District, and may now be seen in the heavy-goods train, whirling onwards at the rate of twelve or fourteen miles an hour, whistling in derision as it passes by the Thames and Canal navigations, and by its speed mocking the drowsy barge (that emblem of the old slowness of traders and the torpid course of their commercial transactions) which would reach the rail train's terminus in four or five days and nights after it, and then return in eight or ten days more, if it escaped being grounded in its passage home.

The Great Western Railway (GWR) was opened from Paddington as far as Maidenhead in 1838, and then to Reading in 1840. A branch line to Henley was opened in 1857. The GWR was a modest contributor to the event which brought it a great deal of traffic. In the peak period of travel just before the Great War, when motor cars were still a novelty, 30,000 passengers were carried to and from London.

Steaming gently past Clivedon in the 1920s is the steamer Hampton Court. *The party in the punt appear to be taking shelter from the steamer's wake. Though steamers were very popular, Charles Dickens and others frowned on them for making life more difficult for self-propelled craft on the upper Thames.*

Once rowing had become popular for sport and pleasure, new boat designs emerged. This is the 'Specialite' Gentleman's pleasure skiff built by E. Messum & Sons of Richmond, Surrey— elevation (below) and plan (opposite).

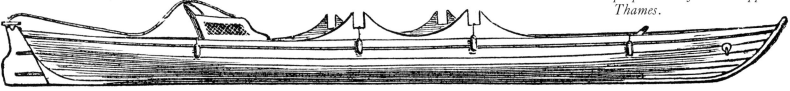

Twenty-six trains were laid on in 1902, signalling systems were changed, a vast army of station staff was drafted in, including twenty-six extra porters, and goods traffic—coal, ballast and chalk trains—was held back to allow the Henley passenger trains a free run.

The first steam trains for the GWR arrived on the line by sea and canal. Two were shipped from Liverpool to London, and then loaded on to barges for West Drayton on the Grand Junction Canal. The *North Star* locomotive came through the London Docks and went up the Thames by barge to Brunel's railway bridge at Maidenhead where it was hoisted on to the track. Thus the river assisted in its own demise, though the populations of up-river towns like Reading and Maidenhead grew fast enough in the railway age for the barge traffic to survive. Coal and other goods were carried throughout the nineteenth century, and some wharves survived until this century.

The coming of the steam barges and tugs in the 1860s, the 'Puffing Billies', and improvements to the locks and dredging of the river, helped to keep commercial traffic going. A measure of the balance between commercial and leisure traffic is provided by the receipts of lock tolls. In 1867, £2,550 came from barges, £1,020 from pleasure craft. By 1887, the position was reversed: far more money came from the pleasure boats.

The great appeal for the Thames at this time is captured and enshrined in Jerome K. Jerome's *Three Men in a Boat*, published in 1889. His characters take the train from London—the author and Harris going from Waterloo, bribing the driver to turn his train into the 11.05 for Kingston. They travel upstream, and when the rowing gets rough they adopt the then popular practice of towing their boat—a great issue in the guide books of the day because amateurs pulling boats tended to get themselves into trouble. 'There is something very strange and unaccountable about a tow-line. You roll it up with as much patience and care as you would take to fold up a new pair of trousers,' writes Jerome, 'and five minutes afterwards, when you pick it up, it is one ghastly tangle.'

You can almost hear the hubbub on the houseboat Stella *at Henley—a wonderfully vivid photograph from the famous Henry Taunt collection.*

In *The Stream of Pleasure—A Month on the Thames*, published in 1891, the Pennells advise:

> *Towing against a strong stream requires more care on the part of the coxswain as well as of the person on the bank than people are generally disposed to believe. A typical accident occurred near the Grotto of Basildon [in Berkshire] on the bank holiday of August 1879, when a boat which was being towed up against a strong flood, and was suddenly steered too far into the stream, was absolutely pulled over by the tow-rope, and capsized.*

A vivid memory of a trip on the river to Henley in the 1930s, when this leisurely era was near its end, is described by Dorothy Deane:

> *An old man in his sixties walked us, or hauled us up the river for a few shillings. Our host, who had been concerned with regattas for fifty or sixty years, arranged this, although thinking now it was a dreadful thing—nobody else was towed. I was with my sister and two men friends. We took a picnic hamper but no alcohol—everyone else was drinking Pimm's. We watched the Henley races from a punt, then we had fireworks in the evening and started off home. We just drifted downstream with Chinese lanterns on the bow, listening to soft music on the gramophone. All the locks were closed so we had to get out and the men had to haul the punt over them. We didn't get back until the early hours of the morning—it was a magical, still night.*

A great variety of boats became popular in the Victorian era, canoes of all kinds, occasional gondolas were seen at Henley, and punting became the fashion. Punts had been fishing boats, as the description given in *Dickens's Dictionary of the Thames* for 1882 makes clear: 'It has at one end an acclivity with cross-bars of wood resembling steps; a well to hold fish alive, about one-third from the other end; the bottom perfectly flat, and the sides bevelled slightly outwards.'

While the art of punting was being perfected, the upper Thames was assailed for the first time by a new contraption of the industrial age—the steam launch. Whereas paddlesteamers were already carrying day-trippers from Westminster or Tower Pier to the estuary resorts from the middle of the century, smaller up-river models had not been developed. Paddlesteamers were too wide to get through the narrow locks, and until the Thames Conservancy had improved the river and cleared it of weed, screw-propeller boats were not a practical possibility because of fouling.

The idyllic image of the Thames at Cliveden in the 1920s when it had become a pleasure resort—the S. S. Steatley glides serenely into Cookham Lock.

A steamer called *Runnymede*, running between Staines and Hampton Court in 1877, is the first recorded service of this kind. By the late nineteenth century, steamers were all over the river, and boat-builders were making them in all shapes and sizes. For those rowing boats or poling punts, these new-fangled boats were a menace. The 1890 edition of *Dickens's Dictionary of the Thames* is scathing:

> *Steam launches are too often the curse of the river. Driving along at an excessive rate of speed, with an utter disregard to the comfort or necessities of anglers, oarsmen, and boating parties, the average steam-launch engineer is an unmitigated nuisance ...*
>
> *Perhaps the worst offenders are the people who pay their £5. 5s. a day for the hire of a launch, and whose idea of a holiday is the truly British notion of getting over as much ground as possible in a given time. Parties of this kind, especially after the copious lunch which is one of the features of the day's outing, stimulate the engineer to fresh exertions, and appear to enjoy themselves considerably as they contemplate the anxiety and discomfort of the occupants of the punts and rowing boats which are left floundering helplessly in their wash.*

Dickens thought the steamer would soon be superseded—by the electric launch. The first of these battery-powered launches appeared in the early 1880s, and in 1889 they were produced commercially. The *Viscountess Bury*, built by Sargent & Co. of Chiswick in 1889 was certified to carry seventy passengers, and was charted by the Prince of Wales for five years for boating trips at Windsor.

Down-river on the Thames tideway, much larger paddlesteamers had established a holiday ritual for Londoners making for Southend-on-Sea (which had an electric railway on its pier in the late nineteenth century), Sheerness and Margate.

Very strangely, however, the greatest and most popular event on the river—followed by crowds on paddlesteamers, cheered from the banks and the bridges—was the annual contest just before Easter between teams from the universities of Oxford and Cambridge. Rowing races, as we have seen, took place from time to time between the two from 1829, but the race did not become a fixed event on the river until 1856. It is rowed over four and a half miles on the flood tide from just above Putney Bridge to just below Chiswick Bridge. The 'Battle of the Blues'—dark blue for Oxford and light blue for Cambridge—once had a much greater following than it does today, dividing the whole of

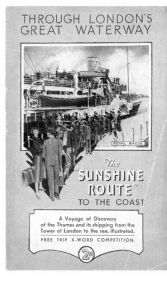

Illustrations from a 'Royal Eagle' paddle-steamer brochure. 'The Sunshine Route' advertised (top) *was the classic holiday for less well-off Londoners, before the package holiday and the motor car took them further afield. One of the attractions of a trip from Westminster Pier down to Southend-on-Sea on a steamer was the variety of shipping in the Port of London* (above).

London and much of the country in their support of two teams, which in social terms meant absolutely nothing to them at all.

It was in 1836—the second race between the two colleges—that the event first took place on the Thames, between Westminster and Putney. Because of the problem of the commercial traffic on the river, it was moved from Westminster to Putney in 1845, after a series of disagreements between the two sides on the timing and rules of the race. One problem was that Cambridge continued to employ a waterman as a coach. Oxford felt this was not in the best interests of rowing as it was developing into a new and pure art form, for watermen persisted with short oar strokes and were inclined to continue with the practice of fouling the opponent, which had been accepted in the watermen's own races as good sport.

'Coxswains must always be trained up from gentlemen,' declared Oxford in a resolution of 1846. 'Nor do watermen even as watermen supply the place of a gentleman coxswain ... they could do no good beyond keeping the men up to their work, they were totally unable to improve individual rowing—a coxswain ought to be a thinking, reasoning being in a higher degree than any watermen have shown themselves to be.'

So watermen disappeared from the race, though they were retained, as they still are, to maintain the boats of the two crews. The social exclusivity of university rowing appears to have had no influence on the broad base of its appeal, which has defied analysis, and is particularly puzzling because the race itself is often a foregone conclusion from early on and rowing is not intrinsically a great spectator sport. The popularity of the race appears to date from quite early on in its history. The *Illustrated London News* reported on 9 April 1881:

> *The popular mind of London yearly gets into a fit of more or less affected excitement upon the favourite occasion that comes off on Friday morning, as usual, along the famous rowing course of the Thames from Putney to Mortlake ... It is not a little remarkable that the declaration of a zealous sympathetic partisanship for one or the other of these learned and revered academical corporations, the two ancient English Universities, should be most frequently uttered by the mouths of babes and sucklings, of servant-maids, errand-boys, and the illiterate streetocracy, who can have no possible reason for partiality to either serene abode of classic studies. 'Are you Oxford or Cambridge?' these simple*

Dad's Navy in action: checking papers on the upper Thames where the riverborne Home Guard was on the look-out for spies and German seaplanes.

folk demand of everyone they meet, as if it were a contested election, when one is supposed to be Liberal or Tory.

However perplexing that may be, the rise of the boat race certainly part of the long transformation of the Thames from a working river to a playground. In particular the upper tideway, above London Bridge, and the non-tidal river above Teddington were entering the modern era well before the Great War.

In wartime, however, the quiet reaches of Henley and Molesey did for a time regain some of their old importance for the nation. A section of the Home Guard was formed, called the Upper Thames Patrol, which was, to all intents and purposes, a kind of 'Dad's Navy'. Equipped with a few rifles and small boats, they prepared for invasion by the Germans, watching out for seaplanes and, like the ancient Britons lined up to repulse Roman invaders, had the task of preventing the enemy from crossing the river. George Kenyon remembers the patrol:

> *We used to have to immobilize all river craft at night in case they could be used by the Germans to get across—we took away the oars, and rowlocks and the floorboards because they could be used for paddling the boat. Open barges were moored in the centre of the river to deter German seaplanes, and we patrolled all the locks on the river because if they were damaged it affected the flow of water and London's water supply intakes were there. At night we used to try to get people to put out the lights on their boats, but they could always hear us coming, and as soon as we'd gone we'd see their lights go on again.*

The upper Thames had in fact become vital to London in the century before war broke out. Not as a highway but as a vital natural resource. Nearly all of the capital's drinking water was pumped out of the river from above Teddington Weir. A well-directed bombing raid or sabotage could have returned London to a more perilous state than it was in the middle of the nineteenth century, when water supply had become one of the most critical issues of the age.

THE THAMES ON TAP

Nobody today would dream of dipping a glass into the Thames next to London Bridge, waiting for the sediment to settle, and then knocking it back to quench their thirst. Yet the river there now is a great deal less polluted than it was around the 1840s when a large part of London's people still got their water supplies directly from the Thames. When the filth from sewers had already killed off the more sensitive fish in the middle Thames and prevented salmon from moving upstream from the sea, private water companies established along the river at Chelsea, Lambeth, York Buildings (Charing Cross) and Bankside were still pumping supplies direct from the Thames to their customers.

In 1850, about twenty years after the last Thames salmon had been caught, Arthur Hill Hassall produced his *A Microscopic Examination of the Water Supplied to the Inhabitants of London and the Suburban Districts*. Of the supplies in Southwark he concluded: 'This water was in the worst condition in which it is possible to conceive any water to be, as regards animalcular contents, in a worse state even than Thames water itself, as taken from the bed of the river ...'

Though the river itself was heavily contaminated with raw sewage and the effluent from gas works, it got *worse* when it was stored in tanks by water companies, and stored again in cisterns in people's houses. Hassall reports of one experiment he carried out: 'A gauze bag, tied to the top of the water cistern is found, at the end of a few days, to contain a mass sufficient to fill an eggshell, consisting principally of the hairs of mammalian animals.'

By the mid-nineteenth century, things were generally improving, but it was a long time before Londoners had anything like the purity and consistency of water supply they have today. Meanwhile, the Thames itself continued to deteriorate. The building of massive sewage pipes north and south of the river in the 1860s carried much of the pollution away from central London. During the twentieth century, the great expansion of London, the use of poor sewage treatment works in semi-detached suburbia, and finally the bombing during the last war which burst pipes and punctured main sewers brought a long-term decline in the river.

Today, the Thames is not exactly drinkable. Our standards in this respect have changed beyond all recognition since the days when, as reported by John Strype in 1750, there might be discussion as to

The Thames at Westminster in the second half of the eighteenth century when London had come to rely more and more on water pumped straight from the river to supply its growing population. The strange tower belongs to York Buildings Waterworks, one of several sited on the river from Chelsea down to London Bridge.

whether the supply from the New River Company was inferior to that pumped from the river at London Bridge because the sediment took longer to settle. An important source of water for the City was from the company which had tidal mills in the arches of Old London Bridge to pump the Thames into storage tanks from where it was distributed to houses. The New River Company brought supplies from near Hertford. Strype says: 'It was observed that the water conveyed into Houses by this Mill [London Bridge] did sooner become fine and clear than the New River Water, and was ever clearer Water, as Mr Charles Hepton that was chief Clerk there hath told me.'

There was certainly a time when the Thames was a great river for fish and better than it is today. However, it is doubtful that it was ever so crystal clear around London Bridge that any modern consumer would consider drinking it, though one might use it to clean the floor or wash the car. The tides which run in from the sea carry with them a suspension of sand and mud which makes the river naturally murky in these parts, just as the most translucent stream will go brown when it floods and erodes the earth on its banks.

As a study of the emergence of an ecological disaster and its slow and painful remedy, there is no better story than what has happened to the Thames over the past two centuries. It is reasonably well documented, at least in its consequences for people and fish. Yet there is a great reluctance today to believe that there is any life in the river, and that it is possible for anything to be done about environmental problems other than an abandonment of our industrial way of life. It is an irony of the great success achieved in cleaning up the river that when there is now a set-back, and the water becomes polluted, large numbers of fish die. There is a story that in 1986 when this happened in a spell of warm weather, MPs debating the problem in the House of Commons looked out of the windows to see shoals of dace, roach, bream and perch belly up in the Thames. What surprised them was that there had been any fish in the river at all at Westminster. Such is the prejudice against belief in the Thames again being a living river.

The history of the river as a source of water and as a fishery is a salutary reminder of how much we now expect in terms of environmental cleanliness, and also of how quickly and easily the Thames could once again be killed off biologically and transformed from a valuable natural resource into a poison. Today about seventy per cent of London's drinking water comes from the upper reaches of the Thames, pumped

Only at the start of this century did most of London have a constant supply of tap-water. In the seventeenth century water carriers were common—this ancient was hawking supplies from the New River Company in the 1680s.

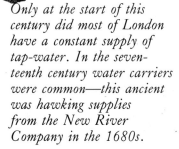

out, filtered and treated. Most of the rest comes from the River Lea, and from deep wells drilled into the layers of chalk and clay in the catchment area. Above Teddington, where the tidal river ends, there have always been fish in the river, but modern sources of pollution, unknown in the nineteenth century, have become a concern— especially the residues of pesticides washed into the Thames from agricultural land.

When London was still a very small town, and the rivers Fleet and Walbrook flowed through the City, it was thought by the standards of the day to be very well supplied with water. On the gravel terraces north of the Thames there were numerous springs, but these were already inadequate in the thirteenth century because of contamination and the increase in population.

The City went in search of new supplies 'for the profit of the City and good of the whole realm ... to wit for the poor to drink and the rich to dress their meat'. According to the sixteenth-century historian Stow, foreign merchants, chiefly French, put up some of the money for laying a lead conduit, or water-pipe, from the River Tyburn to Cheapside in the City. The Tyburn, completely disappeared now, ran through Marble Arch down into the Thames at Westminster.

About half of London's drinking water in the eighteenth century was supplied by the New River—a cleverly constructed channel which brought spring water from Hertfordshire down to a reservoir in Clerkenwell. This was the New River Company's headquarters in 1730—relics of the old reservoir remain on the site, now Thames Water offices.

This was a public supply, free to everyone except tradespeople such as tanners and brewers, who were supposed to pay for their supplies. Only a few people had the right to tap off water into wells in their homes by means of 'quills'. Even at this early date there were complaints about the quality of river water which, according to the Earl of Lincoln in 1297, 'were unfit for drinking due' to filth running into it from tanneries. It seems that Thames water, which was collected either by individuals or by the Company of Water Tankard Bearers of the City, sometimes became salty when there was a low flow of fresh water from up-river. This still happens during droughts because the flow of fresh water is insufficient to hold back the sea water, and shrimps can be found as far inland as Barnes.

The thirteenth-century Tyburn conduit began an intermittent effort to keep London supplied: the River Westbourne was siphoned off for Westminster. Westminster Abbey leased the City springs at Paddington in 1439 for 'two peppercorns' a year, and the pipes from this were extended to Fleet Street by 1471. The street name conduit survives in a number of places, though these water supplies are long gone; for example, Lamb's Conduit Street, named after William Lamb who in 1577 re-built the water-pipe at Holborn.

Meagre though the flow of water was, gravity providing the only force to carry it up to two miles, this was at least a communal supply, and was celebrated annually with a visit to the spring heads at Paddington and Tyburn, where dignitaries tested the water 'and afore Dinner, hunted the hare, and killed her … and after Dinner they went Hunting the fox'. They ran after the beast for a mile, according to an account of 1362, and killed it at St Giles with a 'great Hallowing at his death and Blowing of Horns'.

Conduits provided the main supply until the sixteenth century, when an ingenious Dutchman (some say German), called Peter Morice (or Morris), had the idea of fitting a tidal mill into the northernmost arch of Old London Bridge to pump river water up to the City. To prove that this could be done, Morice fired a jet of water over the steeple of St Magnus the Martyr Church. The first supplies of Thames water began on Christmas Eve 1582.

This was a turning point in London's water supply. The London Bridge Waterworks was a profit-making business, and charged for its supplies. It also introduced the idea of pumping water, which made it possible to tap the River Thames itself, instead of relying on the

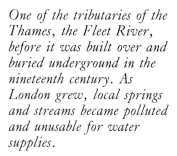

One of the tributaries of the Thames, the Fleet River, before it was built over and buried underground in the nineteenth century. As London grew, local springs and streams became polluted and unusable for water supplies.

Chelsea Waterworks in 1752 showing the beam engine used to pump river water into a reservoir which supplied private households. Some hollowed-out elmwood water pipes—the origin of the term 'trunk communication' —can be seen behind the water cart.

falling gradient of land from tributary streams. There had been one earlier use of a pump to supply a conduit at Dowgate, using horse-powered machinery, but the London Bridge Waterworks—with several wheels working—was the first really successful scheme of its kind. It was destroyed in the Great Fire but re-built, and by the eighteenth century it had four water-wheels which could pump more than one million gallons a day into the City, and a wheel was added on the south side to supply parts of Southwark. In 1809 these waterworks supplied no less than four million gallons a day.

By this time, the original owners of the London Bridge Waterworks had sold out in 1701 to a goldsmith, Richard Soane. In 1821, the company had 10,000 customers paying between £1 and £20 each, according to the amount they received. Water supplies were never constant in those days. The company admitted that the Thames water was 'foul' when it was first pumped out, but after it had stood for twenty-four hours they reckoned it was 'finer than any other water that could be produced'.

Not only were the claims made for Thames water overstated, the London Bridge Waterworks could only supply a local demand. The City was expanding northwards, and an entirely new source was needed. A scheme first proposed in the late sixteenth century was finally begun in 1609: this was to tap springs at Chadwell and Amwell in Hertfordshire and create a channel through which the water would flow into London.

It took more than four years to create this channel, on a carefully worked out plan to ensure the water flowed down a very shallow incline. Sir Hugh Myddelton, a goldsmith and one of the City's Merchant adventurers, took on the task, but he ran out of money half-way through and needed the support of James I to complete the project—the king subsequently taking half the profits until Charles I sold out this right. The New River Company was opened grandly in 1613 at its headquarters in Clerkenwell, which later became the central offices of Thames Water in Rosebery Avenue.

A pond marked the head of the river, and the water from here was distributed to the City in hollowed-out elm logs, sharpened at one end like a pencil, and wedged together. These were standard until iron pipes were introduced in the early nineteenth century. A windmill was used to raise water to a higher reservoir in 1709, then a horse mill, and finally a steam engine in 1768.

The great wheels of London Bridge Waterworks as they were in the eighteenth century. The mill wheels on both the north and south of the river survived until Old London Bridge was demolished in the 1830s, by which time they were supplying millions of gallons of Thames water a day to the City and Southwark.

During the seventeenth century there were new waterworks at Shadwell in East London, York Buildings Works at Charing Cross, and the Hampstead Water Company tapping wells on the Heath. The first two took their supplies from the Thames. The old system of City conduits had been superseded, and they fell into disuse. Water supply had become a commercial business and supplies had to be paid for.

A large proportion of London's poor population had only a communal standpipe: they could not individually afford to pay water rates, and the companies struggling to pay dividends to shareholders could not afford to subsidize them. But even those who had a direct feed into a tank in their home did not get a regular supply in the eighteenth and early nineteenth centuries.

DEMAND FOR WATER INCREASES

London's dependence on Thames water increased greatly in the eighteenth century, not through any preference for it but because alternative supplies were insufficient for its growing population, and the clearer tributary streams—the Westbourne, Tyburn, Fleet and Walbrook in the north, and Effra and Ravensbourne in the south—were being built over and polluted. Its wells too had become contaminated. Commercial water companies which were set up to provide the capital with water at a profit had no alternative but to pump it from the Thames. Remarkably few people found this unacceptable, even in the early 1800s: nobody had made any connection between disease and water supply. The river water itself, at that time, though muddy and disgusting enough by the standards of today, had not been grossly contaminated.

The distribution of water was hampered by the use of wooden pipes which often leaked, and a means of supply which was intermittent and inefficient. In 1756, the London Bridge Waterworks had eight seven-inch pipes running from its water tower; the Chelsea Company had five pipes; and the New River Company no less than fifty-eight pipes, including a main in Goswell Street (now Road), which was nine pipes in parallel. On water days the company's turncock for a street would open up the flow of water which ran into cisterns and buckets in basements: if they were already half-full they overflowed for few people had ballcocks to cut off the supply.

Because there was no pressure in the system, the pipes emptied when the water was turned off. For the early fire brigade this was hopeless because they could draw nothing off: in Soho a well was dug to supply water for fire-fighting after a blaze that could not be put out because the turncock could not be found.

Around the year 1800, about half of London's water came from the River Thames, and about half from the New River Company which had long supplemented its supplies with water from the River Lea.

A balloon view of London at the time of the Great Exhibition in 1851 (opposite) *when much of the capital's water supply still came from the Thames in the centre of London.*

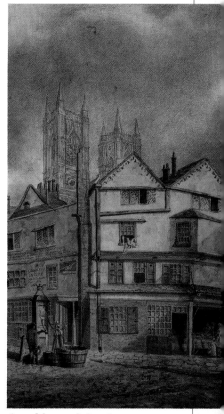

An old standpipe in Westminster in 1805 (above). *Once conduits had provided water free, but by this period only the poor used this supply because they could not afford the charges of the water companies.*

The population was growing at a tremendous pace: it had been 700,000 in the 1770s, and was by 1801 near to a million. In some districts the population rose in the same period from a few hundred people to tens of thousands. The figures for St Pancras were 600 to 32,000. The demand for water was rising not only because of the rise in population, but also because of change in habits. People were wearing cotton clothes which were washed more often; a larger number of households had washbasins and fixed baths; and, most important of all, the flush toilet, or water closet, had arrived.

Although the water companies were by this time pumping millions of gallons from the Thames, wastage through leakages (up to a quarter of the total) and the increasing demand for water made it impossible for the companies with their water-mills, gravity-fed, wooden pipes, and unpressured supplies to keep pace.

The great concern at that time, as John Graham-Leigh has pointed out ('The Transformation of London's Water Supply 1805–1821', unpublished thesis), was with getting *more* water, not with the quality of supplies. The story of how London eventually got a decent water supply, and was freed from reliance on the fetid Thames is fascinating and Byzantine in its detail. Only a rough sketch can be given here of the way in which the kind of supply we expect today was achieved. It involved fierce competition between rival water companies, technological advance with the design of steam engines, innumerable government inquiries and the passing of laws to regulate the way in which private companies operated until the Metropolitan Water Board was set up in 1902 and the first public authority took over.

As London expanded in the early 1800s, new water companies arose to serve the outlying districts: there was the South London Waterworks of 1805, the East London Waterworks of 1807, the West Middlesex Waterworks of 1806 and the Grand Junction Waterworks Company of 1811. Though they began by supplying new districts, these companies soon began to compete for customers with the old established works. There was fierce and often ridiculous rivalry, with two companies laying mains along the same street, but the new companies began to dominate, principally because they were using better technology.

Steam engines had been used since the mid-eighteenth century to pump water out of the Thames and up into cisterns or reservoirs from where the supply was gravity fed to consumers. These engines became

The revolting state of London's drinking water, pumped untreated and unfiltered from the river into people's homes from a river which was also a sewer, satirized in Punch.

THE WATER THAT JOHN DRINKS.

THIS is the water that JOHN drinks.

This is the Thames with its cento of stink,
That supplies the water that JOHN drinks.

These are the fish that float in the ink-
-y stream of the Thames with its cento of stink,
That supplies the water that JOHN drinks

This is the sewer, from cesspool and sink,
That feeds the fish that float in the ink-
-y stream of the Thames with its cento of stink,
That supplies the water that JOHN drinks.

These are vested int'rests, that fill to the brink,
The network of sewers from cesspool and sink,
That feed the fish that float in the ink-
-y stream of the Thames, with its cento of stink,
That supplies the water that JOHN drinks.

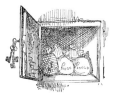

This is the price that we pay to wink
At the vested int'rests that fill to the brink,
The network of sewers from cesspool and sink,
That feed the fish that float in the ink-
-y stream of the Thames with its cento of stink,
That supplies the water that JOHN drinks.

much more efficient later in the century, particularly with the innovations of Watt and Boulton. Beam engines, developed for pumping out water from Cornish tin and copper mines, were also installed, replacing horse gins, windmills and less powerful steam engines. At the same time, iron pipes began to replace hollowed-out elm trunks. Once the problem of making waterproof joins in the pipes was solved, an entirely new system was feasible as water could be pumped into reservoirs at a higher pressure.

The most successful of the new suppliers, the East London Waterworks Company, opened its Old Ford Works on 23 October 1809. It had laid twenty miles of iron pipes, brought from Sheffield by canal to the east coast, and then by sea to London. Two Boulton and Watt engines pumped water from the River Lea. There was a stand for spectators at the opening ceremony, attended by dignitaries of the East India Company and the Lord Mayor of London. The bands of the First Tower Hamlets Militia and the Loyal Bow Volunteers played 'God Save the King', 'Rule Britannia' and 'Water Parted from the Sea', and there was a sermon on the theme of 'Thou shalt smite the rock, and there shall come water out of it, that the people may drink.'

Water supply rather than quality was still the big issue. Ralph Dodd, an engineer and promoter of water companies (most of which threw him out at an early stage of development), wrote in 1805:

> *Thames water being kept in wooden vessels, after a few months, often becomes putrid ... and produces a disagreeable smell. But even when drunk in this state, it never produces sickness; therefore it is evident no harm or ill occurs to persons whose resolution, notwithstanding its offensive smell, induces them to drink it.*

Within thirty years, medical opinion on that matter was utterly changed, and the appalling state of the water available to Londoners—the poor in particular—had become a lively public issue. This was before the first epidemic of Asiatic cholera in 1832, which is believed to have killed 5,300 Londoners as it spread through Rotherhithe, Southwark, Lambeth, Limehouse and Ratcliffe, reaching Marylebone and Hoxton. Nobody understood the nature of the disease then, and doctors disagreed on the cause of contagion. It was only later in the century when the detective work of men like John Snow—who mapped the locations of outbreaks in cholera years and related them to particular sources of water—finally established a firm link with drinking water.

A satirical print from 1832, showing the owner of Southwark Waterworks sitting on a chamber pot—the theme of Londoners drinking raw sewage was often repeated in this period.

The weight of medical opinion and further cholera outbreaks, principally in 1848–49, led to new laws forcing the water companies to get cleaner water. By the time most of the older companies had folded or been absorbed into new ones, fixed territories had been set up to avoid wasteful competition and new ways of purifying water had been pioneered. London Bridge Waterworks, which had been taken over by the New River Company, closed down when the bridge was demolished in the 1830s, but the New River Company itself survived.

A Metropolis Water Act of 1852 was the turning point. From then on no water could be drawn from the Thames below Teddington Weir; all supplies had to be filtered; and service reservoirs within five miles of St Paul's had to be covered over. The water companies now set up their pumping stations on the relatively clean upper reaches of the river, and they had the steam power, the iron pipes, and the know-how to feed it into London.

There were further cholera epidemics in 1853–54. In east London, where many poor people remained without decent supplies of water until late in the century, there was an epidemic in 1866. But by the 1870s a recognizably modern form of supply, with taps and wash-basins and baths, was coming into existence and constant running water arrived between 1871 and 1899.

Around the turn of the century the problem of water supply had essentially been solved, and the process of purification started to evolve. It was found that the storage of water in reservoirs before supplies were filtered improved its quality immensely. Between 1900 and the Great War the large Staines reservoirs were created and many other storage reservoirs have been built since then. During the war the pumping of water into these reservoirs was made difficult by a shortage of coal and pre-chlorination was tried, using bleaching powder to kill off bacteria.

Today London gets two-thirds of its water from the Thames. It is pumped into storage reservoirs, from there through treatment plants, and on to service reservoirs which are covered over and hardly noticed by anyone. From these it is largely gravity fed into homes.

The water closet had been invented back in the sixteenth century by Sir John Harrington and was fitted to one house in the City. At Greenwich and Richmond royal palaces there were sewers which ran into the river, but nobody else had a domestic sewage or waste pipe. The

MICROCOSM · dedicated to the London Water Companies · "BROUGHT FORTH ALL MONSTROUS, ALL PRODIGIOUS THINGS, HYDRAS, AND GORGONS, AND CHIMERAS DIRE." Vide Milton

MONSTER SOUP commonly called THAMES WATER, being a correct representation of that precious stuff doled out to us !!!

underground sewage system, such as it was, took the surface water from the streets. Most Londoners simply had chamber pots which were emptied into cesspits which night-soil men, or 'dong fermers' in early parlance, emptied, taking the contents out to the market gardens which fed London. In Lincoln's Inn privies opened on to the chimney shafts. One of the few public toilets was on Old London Bridge, a hazard no doubt for passing watermen.

Though science and medicine had begun to understand the relationship between filthy water and disease in the 1820s, official complacency remained. 'Monster Soup' is a satire from 1827.

The building of Crossness sewage works, which was part of the grand scheme to carry London's effluent downstream in the 1860s. It made the river healthier for Londoners, but did little for the fish and wildlife of the Thames below London Bridge.

Water closets need sewers: a cesspit would soon fill up with the volume of water going through, but they became fashionable before proper sewers were built. As a result they were connected to existing sewers, which of course ran straight into the river. The sewage was often discharged at the very same spot on the Thames where the water was pumped out to supply houses with their domestic water, and that for their new flush toilet.

It must be remembered that half of London's water was coming from the river, and none of it—until the Chelsea Waterworks Company pioneered a scheme in 1829—was even filtered, never mind purified in the modern sense.

However, until new sources of water could be found, there was nothing the growing metropolis could do. All kinds of schemes were

put forward, both for carrying the sewage further out of town, and for creating rainwater lakes around London to do away with reliance on the Thames. The problem of pollution was made worse by the fact that the river was tidal, which meant that putrid water was carried up and down the river twice a day, and took a long time to reach the sea. In fact, quite a lot of discharged sewage would be carried *up-river* on the flow of the tide only to sweep back through London on the ebb.

Victorian steam pump technology was employed to take sewage out of central London. An Act of 1855 set up the Metropolitan Board of Works, the chief purpose of which was: 'to construct a system of sewerage which should prevent all or any part of the sewage within the metropolis from passing into the Thames in or near the metropolis'. For the first time, London had a powerful local government body, and was able to tackle the problem on a grand scale.

The new board's chief engineer was Joseph Bazalgette. His scheme for dealing with sewage was astonishingly bold and, generally, successful. Massive brick tunnels were dug right through north and south London, incorporating the new embankments in the centre of town, with pumping stations to raise the flow of sewage where gravity failed. Existing sewers which had run directly into the Thames were intercepted by massive new sewage pipes which took the effluent out to Beckton in the north and Crossness in the south. Here the sewage was stored to be discharged into the river at high tide.

It was raw sewage going into the Thames, rather than industrial pollution from tanneries and factories along the river, which had begun to kill off the fish at a time when half the metropolis was drinking a diluted form of their own excrement. The solution to the problem of water supply, which came from the mid-nineteenth century onwards, did something for the wildlife of the river, but not enough to save the fisheries. Whereas Londoners were in time freed from the necessity of using water from the river in the built-up areas, and could find cleaner sources up-river, the fish and other creatures, of course, could not.

Although central London had a cleaner river, the Thames itself remained filthy and the problem for migratory fish had not changed. Evidence taken by a Royal Commission in the early 1800s heard of river pilots suffering from nausea and headaches because of the smell. Fish caught in the estuary or the sea and carried in 'live wells' up to Billingsgate were dying as they came through the Beckton reaches.

One of the south London sewage pipes built in the Victorian period and still in use today.

By the Maior.

Orders devised and agreed upon by the Right Honourable Sir *Robert Ducie*, Knight and Baronet, Lord Maior of the City of *London*, and Confervator of the River of *Thames* and Waters of *Medway*, for the Prefervation of the Brood and Fry of Fifh within the Weft part of the faid Rivers, as followeth.

Until the end of the eighteenth century, there were thriving fisheries in the Thames at places such as Fulham and Chelsea where salmon were caught in season. This is a Bill for the preservation of fisheries from the records of the City Corporation which was the conservator of the river until the mid-nineteenth century.

In the early 1800s, there was a sizeable fishing industry on the Thames. The City Corporation was the fishing authority from Staines down to the estuary, issuing licences and regulations on the size of nets permitted and closed seasons for particular species. In the City archives are records of fishermen from Erith, Rainham and Dagenham being prosecuted for using too small a mesh in their nets, which were publicly burned at Cheapside in the fourteenth century. Fishermen from Chiswick, Petersham and Fulham were also prosecuted.

A great variety of fishing techniques were used along the river, with traps and nets the names of which are a roll-call of long-forgotten skills: petersnets, pridents, treinkes, chotnet, gorce and kidel. Such was the importance of the industry in the fifteenth century, and the concern that the river would be over-fished, that bailiffs clashed violently with fishermen. There is a tale in 1407 of a bailiff being pursued as he made off with illegal nets down-river to Barking to hand them over to constables, and many arrows being fired at him. Aldermen were assailed with arrows in 1454 while removing an illegal fish weir at Northfleet.

The fishermen were generally poor, using peterboats which were about twenty-two feet long, sometimes with a sail, and with a well to hold fish alive. They would sell their catch at Billingsgate. But what were they fishing for?

A tidal river like the Thames has a great variety of fish. Near the estuary there are sole, cod, herring, sprat and the young of the last two, whitebait. Because the river has both salt and fresh water, it is home to what are known as euryhaline fish, those which can tolerate both conditions. Flounder breed in the southern North Sea, but their young, about the size of postage stamps, move up river on the tides to feed in fresh water. Sizeable fish can be found right in the centre of London. Smelt, a small silvery fish related to the salmon, migrate within the estuary. They spawn up-river at places like Hammersmith, and the young move downstream as they grow. Eels spawn in the Atlantic near Bermuda, and the young move east on the ocean currents. And of course, there is the most celebrated migratory fish of all, the salmon, which seeks out the shallows way inland to breed.

Fish move up and down the Thames rather like shipping, and the seasons for catching them correspond very much to their movements. In the higher reaches of the river, the young or parr of salmon and trout were caught in great quantities and known as 'skeggers'. There

was, until the nineteenth century, a considerable salmon fishing industry on the Thames, but the often repeated story that it was such a common food that apprentices rioted because they were given too much, or that their indentures specified they should not be given it more than once a week, is a myth. Why this story is so popular is a mystery: it probably has something to do with a desire to believe in a golden age before industry spoiled the abundance of the natural world. Extensive research in the 1950s uncovered no documentation for this story, and all the evidence of the price salmon fetched in London shows it to have been a very expensive fish. Demand often outstripped supply for there are records of salmon being brought to London from Perth in Scotland as early as 1334. The Thames would never have

Thames fishermen casting their nets near Vauxhall Bridge in 1821, around the time the river was beginning to die because of sewage pollution as a result of the popularity of the flush toilet.

been the best of Britain's salmon rivers. As a lowland river it had fewer spawning grounds than the Wye, Usk or Severn which rise in mountainous regions. Its rich variety of fish would also have provided fierce competition for the young salmon in the upper river.

The season for Thames salmon was March to September when the adults were running up from the sea. There were fisheries at Wandsworth, at Chelsea where the Lord of the Manor had the rights from Battersea to Lambeth, at Putney and at Fulham. In fact Fulham was a fishing village until the early nineteenth century, and in 1766 there is a record of 130 salmon being sent from there in one day. The salmon fishery was still very active in the late nineteenth century, the catch varying from one year to another, depending on the run of fish, but the catches began to decline steeply in the early 1800s. One reason for this was the building of new locks and weirs, particularly at Teddington (1812), which made it easier to catch the migrating fish and made their up-river journey more difficult. Improvements which were made for navigation of the river, the removal of shallows and the building of locks would also have reduced spawning grounds. The final blow, however, was the invention of the water closet and the gross pollution of the river by sewage.

Salmon are sensitive fish in that they need a high level of dissolved oxygen in the water to survive. Organic pollution breeds bacteria which consume the oxygen. Although the migrating fish did not stay in the most polluted parts of the river, they had to get through London, and the great mass of stinking, oxygen-less water moving up and down with the tides killed them or drove them back. By the 1830s the fisheries were gone and there were hardly any records of salmon, except in the estuary. A remarkable record of catches made by a fishing family, the Lovegroves at Boulter's Lock between 1794 and 1821, charts the decline: the figures were presented to the Salmon Fisheries Commission of 1861, by which time there were no fish left. Between the first year of records and 1810 the catch varied from fifteen to sixty-six in the peak of 1801. In 1812, there were eighteen; 1819, five; 1820, none; and one in 1821. By the end of the period large salmon were fetching 6s. a pound. In 1824, the last salmon was caught at Boulter's Lock and they were not seen again for 150 years.

Another less well known but arguably more important fish in the Thames was killed off by pollution. Smelt were caught in large numbers as they migrated up the river to breed from March to May. They

A girl selling eels in London in the eighteenth century—the Thames was full of this delicacy then. Eels have now returned to the river, with a run of young or elvers each spring, and they are fished commercially.

are delicious fish which smell of cucumber when they first come out of the water. When abundant they could be hauled out like sprats for they grow to only ten inches in length. City records from the end of the eighteenth century testify to the importance of this fish for Londoners. There was a petition to the Lord Mayor in February 1798:

> The season of the year being uncommonly forward, and in consequence, the Smelts which are seldom fit to take till the beginning of April, being now in the Thames in large quantities, several persons, deputed by the main body of Fishermen, applied to the Lord Mayor ... to allow them to begin fishing for Smelts immediately in place of waiting till the 25th of March ...

It was said that the smelt fishing when it began would employ 500 people. Yet in his book *A History of British Fishes*, published posthumously in 1859, a London stationer and naturalist William Yarrell recorded:

> Formerly, the Thames from Wandsworth to Putney Bridge, and from thence upwards to ... the bridge of Hammersmith, produced an abundance of smelts, and from thirty to forty boats might then be seen working together, but very few are now to be taken, the state of the water it is believed, preventing the fish advancing so high up.

In years when there was a high flow of water from up-river, the smelt continued to get through, and a few were caught later in the nineteenth century, but commercial fishery appears to have been dead by 1850.

Another important fishery which was not wiped out, but was severely reduced by pollution, was the trapping of eels. From November to January wicker eel-bucks, like baskets, were put across the Thames and its tributaries to catch mature eels moving back to the sea on their long journey to their breeding grounds across the Atlantic. Between March and June the arriving young eels or elvers moved in a swarming mass up the river and were taken in great quantities.

Eels were less affected than salmon or smelt by pollution. They can tolerate water with less oxygen—in fact they can move over land. Elvers will climb over locks and other obstacles in their nocturnal migrations. Attempts to count numbers of elvers in the nineteenth century recorded between 600 and 1,600 each minute passing a thread drawn across the river. However, by the 1860s, the migration of elvers through London appears to have been severely reduced by the effects of pollution.

The caption from this seventeenth-century 'Cries of London' reads, 'Buy my flounders', but the fish in the basket look more like smelt, a little fish which migrates within the Thames estuary and is related to the salmon. Flounders were common too. Both species now live and breed in the river again, moving right through the centre of town.

Dr Albert Gunther of the Natural History Museum in London did some experiments in the mid-nineteenth century with fish kept in tanks of water with variable concentrations of sewage. He floated cages of eels, flounder and shrimp on the ebb tide below Beckton and noted how long they took to die. Those at the bottom of the cage were mostly killed in about thirty-five minutes. No fish lived between Beckton and Purfleet in Dr Gunther's estimation, though a few flounder made it through to the upper river.

Though the fish population of the tidal Thames and its tributaries was badly affected by pollution in the mid-nineteenth century, and the salmon disappeared, it is a remarkable fact that the river was in a much worse condition in the centre of London a century later.

In the 1880s sewage treatment works cleaned up the outflow, and the river seems to have improved a little up to the Great War. But between the wars, when London's area doubled with the building of semi-detached suburbia, ineffective sewage works put poor quality outflows back into the river and it deteriorated again.

Bomb damage to sewage pipes during the Second World War made things worse, so that by the 1950s the River Thames in the centre of town was at least as bad as, if not worse than it had ever been.

A survey conducted in the 1950s by Alwyne Wheeler of the Natural History Museum found no fish life in the Thames for forty-eight miles between Kew and Gravesend. To reach this conclusion he made extensive inquiries of fishermen and other authorities, including river police and dockers. Mysteriously, given the absence of oxygen, eels sometimes turned up. These, it seems, were stragglers from re-stocking experiments up-river: there was no run of elvers at this time.

In the mid-1960s, when the river stank horribly in hot weather, a committee investigated, and the Port of London Authority and the London County Council (LCC) set about improving the purification of the main sewage works and cutting down industrial pollution. The biggest problem was still the lack of oxygen in the water due to bacteria living on the sewage. Their aim was to get dissolved oxygen levels back up again so that salmon might migrate once more and fish could live in the river.

The first signs of success came in March 1964, and in the most bizarre way. A new power station was being built at West Thurrock, and an engineer working on the screens which filtered debris from the river water which was pumped in for cooling found a tadpole-fish. It

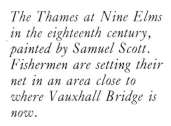

The Thames at Nine Elms in the eighteenth century, painted by Samuel Scott. Fishermen are setting their net in an area close to where Vauxhall Bridge is now.

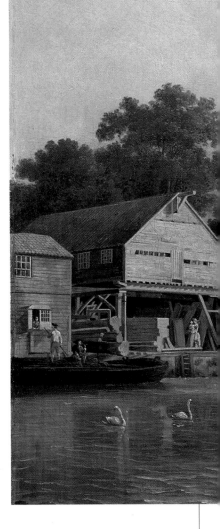

was an odd specimen so he sent it to Alwyne Wheeler for identification. This species was unusual for the southern North Sea—but it was remarkable that anything had been found there alive. The engineer, a Mr Coleman, agreed to keep any other finds, and soon a sand goby, a stickleback and a lampern turned up.

There were many power stations, all with one or another kind of cooling water screen, sited along the Thames then—Ford's own plant

at Dagenham, Barking, Blackwall Point, Brunswick Wharf, Battersea, Lombard Road and Fulham. Alwyne Wheeler developed a survey of the returning fish by organizing a collection of fish on these screens. In addition, the LCC's successor, the Greater London Council, organized fishing competitions, and a number of samples were successfully netted.

In November 1974 Wheeler was called to examine a salmon caught in the screens at West Thurrock power station. It was in a poor state, but still alive. There was great excitement in the Press, although someone dismissed the historic event by claiming they recognized this salmon from a newspaper photograph and they had thrown it into the Thames after keeping it in their deep freeze! That unwillingness to believe in life in a once dead river continues.

Salmon had great publicity value, and, when it was realized they might return, the Thames Water Authority set up a re-stocking programme. It did not have an immediate success—the parr have to turn to smolt which then move down to the sea where they might spend two to four years before they return. By 1988 adult salmon were running up the river once again—more than 300 were recorded at Molesey. The greatest problem for the salmon now is getting past all the locks and weirs on the upper river, but a Salmon Trust is building fish ladders to help them reach their spawning grounds.

So far, 109 species of fish have been recorded in the Thames since the clean-up. The smelt are back, spawning near Hammersmith. Baby flounder move up on the tides. The first elvers turned up at West Thurrock in 1968, and by the late 1970s they were once again migrating in large numbers.

The eel fishery returned, and was doing well, once again supplying Billingsgate Market, when scientists from the Ministry of Agriculture, Fisheries and Food found a concentration of the pesticide dieldrin in samples from the Thames.

An entirely new set of pollution problems had emerged in the post-war period, concentrated much more on what was getting into the river above Teddington. In particular, the dowsing of farmland with chemicals since the 1950s has threatened to contaminate London's water supplies. And there is the horrifying thought that, with the great growth of towns on the upper reaches which pump their sewage into the river, those in the centre of town are drinking water that has been drunk five times (that is the usual figure given) already.

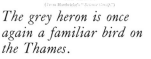

THE HERON.
(From Hardwicke's "Science Gossip.")

The grey heron is once again a familiar bird on the Thames.

Although the river was far less clean than it is today, it was a popular resort for boys living in Wapping and Rotherhithe earlier this century.

Some treated sewage goes into the river above the central London intakes, but it is a tiny proportion of the flow of water. And of course all the water extracted from the river is treated before it is supplied. However, the vogue for drinking mineral water appears to be in part a reaction to contemporary fears about what might be in tap water. The threat of cholera or infection is far from the minds of Londoners today: they are more anxious about poisoning from industrial pollution.

NATURE ON THE THAMES

As to the wildlife of the upper Thames, the fish still thrive. Today you can catch dace, a lovely silvery freshwater fish, just by Westminster Bridge. Salmon once again make the journey up through the estuary, under Tower Bridge, past Parliament, all the way to Teddington and beyond in search of their old spawning grounds.

Following the fish are sea-birds. Not so much the black-headed gulls which winter in large flocks in London—they feed more on the rubbish tips and in the parks. One of the most familiar birds, looking almost pre-historic in its black silhouette, is the cormorant. Herons hunt by the outflow of West Thurrock Power Station, where the fish caught in the filters are fed back into the river.

The massive increase in pleasure boats has churned up the river, eroded the banks and made it a much less hospitable place for birds like the great crested grebe which nest close to the water's edge. Anglers' lead weights were swallowed by swans which died from poisoning in large numbers, but with the ban on lead tackle, they are now returning. However, the biggest impact on wildlife has come from the growth of towns along the river. Large areas of towns such as Maidenhead have been built on the flood plain of the Thames, and efforts to control the river have progressively removed one of the best habitats for wildlife. Places like Port Meadow, close to Oxford, are regularly covered in water each winter, and are feeding grounds for geese, plover, and other wading birds like redshank. In the constantly evolving effort to right past wrongs, the National Rivers Authority (now the new conservator of the river) is trying to create artificial flood plains which drain off the overflow into areas safe for riverside dwellers, and useful for wintering birds and marsh-loving plants.

The Thames itself remains a great and powerful force, and the threat of a flood still hangs over the whole of London. It is to this that the last chapter is devoted.

The return of the fish-eating cormorant is proof enough that the river is alive again in central London.

The beach by Tower Bridge in the 1940s. It seems quite unbelievable now, but an official bathing place was opened here in 1934 and was used until the 1950s, despite serious pollution of the river.

A STRONG BROWN GOD

In the *Four Quartets*, the poet T. S. Eliot has a few verses about 'the river' which capture its timeless, menacing nature. He sees it as a 'strong brown god ... keeping his seasons and rages, destroyer, reminder of what men choose to forget'. It is first a frontier, then a commercial highway, a problem for bridge-builders—then the 'brown god is almost forgotten'. But it is 'waiting, watching, and waiting'.

From the very earliest times, the Thames has flooded its banks, destroying buildings and drowning people and livestock. It has done so from the estuary all the way up to its highest reaches: the record of its seasons and rages go back to the Roman period. But mostly it is a benign river, flowing sweetly between its banks, and carrying ships far inland on the powerful drag of its daily tides. It is good and unmenacing for such long periods of time that those who live along its banks forget how dangerous it can be, and they build their homes on its flood plains in Oxfordshire and Berkshire and on the salt marshes of the estuary, shoring up the banks after each alarming inundation and ignoring its potential power until the next time the waters rise, and go on rising until the defensive walls are breached.

When the floods do come they are always a surprise, and in no two floods, whether on the tidal river or inland, has the river behaved in quite the same way. Within living memory there have been terrible disasters, the greatest of which occurred on the night of 31 January 1953. A large part of East Anglia was flooded by a great North Sea tide, and the people of Canvey Island on the Thames estuary were devastated when the sea breached some old defences and rushed in on their homes, many of which were cheaply built and turned over when the stilts that supported them were washed away.

Though the tides washed around Canvey Island every day, and those who lived there might have expected a disaster, there was no effective flood warning system and everyone was caught completely by surprise. The testimony of those who survived the nightmare on 31 January captures the horror of the sudden tidal flood. Bernard Griffiths has a vivid recollection of his experience:

> *On the night of 31 January 1953, I was MCing at a dance in the Admiral Jellicoe for the Railway Travellers Association. After the dance a crowd of us went back to a local school teacher's caravan for a coffee. Then we heard the sirens, we thought,*

The classic view of the Thames as a great, benign river, painted by Canaletto in the mid-eighteenth century. But even then the tides would sometimes rise way above expected levels and flood London.

Oh that must be some fire, and took no more notice. When I left, I noticed that a dip in the road was filled with water. We shouted out to a fella standing by the side of the road, 'That was some fire!' He said, 'Oh no mate, it wasn't a fire, the island's flooded'. Then my car cut out so I set off home in my wellingtons, saying to the others, 'Hope you get home alright.' On my way home the water was fairly deep, so I tried to get up on to the sea wall, I suddenly found myself waist deep in water. I tried to get to Joe's as I knew he had a boat, the water was getting deeper. I got to his flat which was a second floor flat above a grocer's shop. He was worried about his sister so we set off to see if she was OK. When we got there it was obvious she wasn't there, we tried other friends, but she was lost, drowned.

Then we went to check if my auntie and uncle were alright who lived in Newlands Road. We saw an elderly gentleman on the roof of his garage in a terrible state so we picked him up. People were calling out for help all over the place. We banged on the roof just in case they were inside, but there was no answer. So we started going round picking up as many people as we could. There was a lady standing on the roof of her bungalow who implored us to rescue her husband who had a heart condition, the only way we could get to him was to rip the tiles off the roof with our bare hands until we managed to get to him. Then we heard this man in a terrible state with his little boy, his wife and a baby were drowned, we wanted to just take him and the boy, but he insisted we take his wife too. So I covered her up with my mac and rowed them to a houseboat nearby with the other survivors. When we went back to help some other people, it was getting light, we heard a woman screaming, we traced it to a little bungalow, the water was down to about six foot by then, we looked through the top window and we saw a woman standing there on a sideboard hanging on to a picture rail by her hands. We managed to get the window open, climb through and on to a table in the room and get hold of her. Then we took her back to the houseboat.

The next day, I went round to my auntie and uncle's in a canoe, it was hard to get back on to the island. I found their bodies. My auntie's body was lying on a chair which had fallen over, she had her arm wedged through the back of the chair, my

uncle was on the floor underneath her. The police took them away. I stayed on the island to help with sandbagging for the rest of the week.

Reg Stevens, the surveyor with Canvey Council, found himself with the responsibility of organizing the rescue operation, but it was difficult to convince those in power that a disaster was happening:

The night of 31 January, it was very cold, a howling gale. At about twenty past midnight, I was knocked up by the local police sergeant who told me that he was getting reports of water coming over the sea walls at various parts of the island.

As I made my way to the council offices, I looked over the wall to the Thames, it was absolutely calm, the wind was blowing off-shore in a north-westerly direction, there was a full moon reflected in the still water, then I began to realize that the northern part of the island really would be in trouble.

When I got back to the offices I decided to warn the islanders, we used the old wartime siren used to call out the fire brigade hoping that some people in the vicinity would hear this and realize that a disaster was happening. They also fired maroons, to

Canvey Islanders being rescued by boat during the floods of 1953 (above left). A tidal surge devastated a large part of East Anglia and the Thames estuary, and almost reached London.

Searching for survivors in flooded houses at Canvey Island in 1953 (above right).

Showbery

Prickelwell

Lee

Towle ness

Black tayle

Wakiringe

Lee timbars

Showbery ness

Warpe

Chapman

Midle grounde

Red sande

Pote hauon   Scars

The River of

Wil Jenben

Noure

Lode s

Grayne

Shœrness

Mmstar

Stoknorthe

Belsdore

Qumbrough

Castell

SHEPE

Stocfhere

Sharp ness

Oten Point

Moushoule

Grean ness

Hoo

Cockam Woode

Crosse ness

Damlet pomt

Foule pet

Queenes ferry

Ret ferry

Epnor Castell

Upchurche

cusbery

Renan

Jenam Creeke

Gillioham

Conneyent Creeke

Chatham

Morton

Rocheffer

I   II   III   IIII   V   VI

make as much noise as possible, but the wind was howling so much it was difficult really for a noise to reach very far.

I dispatched my staff to do a reconnaissance of the extent of the breaches in the sea wall, and I went off to the areas where I feared the worst, Newlands, Sunken Marsh and the Sixty Acres. There in the moonlight, I saw people clinging on to the roofs of properties, some bodies, people who unfortunately had been drowned already, one man spreadeagled in a tree, quite a horrifying sight.

The telephone system on Canvey was a manual exchange, I was able to get through to the operator to persuade him to give me priority for any calls. He was absolutely magnificent, he sat literally in water gradually increasing in depth until the telephone system went out of operation, he kept my calls going for as long as was humanly possible. When the exchange went out of operation, our only contact with the mainland was the local ambulance radio on which I could call the ambulance headquarters at Chelmsford, it had been fitted only the week before.

Eventually I managed to get a message to Sir Bernard Braine, our local MP, who did a great deal in organizing rescue operations from the Chelmsford end. It was really difficult to persuade people that there was a major disaster, it was two o'clock on a Sunday morning, and the Essex police had already been inundated with problems from all parts of Essex. There had been flooding already in Jaywick and Clacton.

In 1953 there was no effective flood warning system for Canvey Island. The London authorities had a warning system arranged with the Southend Pier authorities, and the River Authority had a system based at Harwich which should have been conveyed to Canvey. But as far as the local council was concerned, they were not part of any warning system in 1953. Nobody had, anyway, predicted the height the tide would reach.

In retrospect it appears quite remarkable how reluctant the people of Canvey Island were to accept that they were about to be engulfed by the sea that night, despite all the signs that something exceptional was happening. Canvey had been reclaimed from tidal marshland in the Middle Ages, and it lies below the level of spring tides behind its defensive walls. Like much of the east coast and the Thames estuary, it is exceptionally vulnerable to flooding, and before the tidal surge

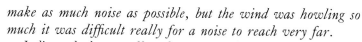

The Thames estuary in the sixteenth century: since then sea levels, and the highest tides, have risen.

reached Canvey in 1953 it had already inundated places further north. Some of the tide gauges had been swept away and right down the east coast from Scotland there were reports that the tide was running much higher than predicted.

But there had been many warnings before which had come to nothing. It was a case of 'cry wolf'. Not only the people of Canvey, but those in towns along the east coast were caught out. Recent research on people's perception of flood dangers suggest that memories are short—if there have been no disasters for a while, everyone forgets or imagines conditions have changed, and the problem has been solved.

However, in the last few years there has been a heightened awareness in London about the dangers of a rise in sea levels which might make the present defences, including the Thames Barrier which is less than a decade old, obsolete and useless. Everyone has learned about the threat of global warming, the melting of ice caps, the hole in the ozone layer, and the evils of the greenhouse effect brought on by the forces of industrialization. The wilder conservationist groups have couched their pronouncements about the imminent demise of London itself in almost biblical terms, as if the flood that threatens is retribution for our tampering with the natural world.

It is as well to get these millennial notions into some kind of perspective, and to distinguish between the various kinds of flooding that occur on the river. The Thames Barrier does nothing to protect those who live below it towards the sea, and has no influence inland beyond the tidal reaches of the Thames. Not everyone understands this, for a survey of people in Eton Wick near Maidenhead found about a quarter who thought the barrier would prevent flooding there. Others were indignant when the Thames overflowed its banks in the winter of 1990.

Some reaches of the river between its source and the sea are more vulnerable to flooding than others, but the danger is there right along the length of the river. Exceptional rainfall or a rapid melting of snow provides the threat to places in the Thames valley down to Molesey. From there to the sea, though a rush of fresh water might make conditions worse, the chief threat is from exceptionally high tides. The way those tides behave affects the vulnerability of different places—the 1953 tidal surge did not flood central London, but a high tide in 1928 did.

Freshwater flooding and tidal flooding have quite different causes, and though they might work together to increase the danger to London it is as well to consider them separately. It is also important to

In 1928, the Thames overflowed its banks in central London—here a child is being rescued in Rotherhithe.

understand that the greatest potential disaster that could occur on the Thames would be for the river to overflow its banks in the centre of London. The capital would be paralysed, and a study in the 1960s which considered the value of a flood barrier warned that the death and destruction could easily overshadow that of the Blitz. This is not to belittle the misery flooding can cause in the upper reaches or on the estuary, but to get into perspective the special nature of the threat to central London.

It is a tidal flood which could devastate London, and the scale of threatened disaster has been increasing steadily over the centuries as the metropolis has grown and the Thames has risen higher and higher between its banks. The river is much deeper and narrower than in Roman times. The high-water levels at London Bridge have increased steadily: whereas it was under 14 ft in 1791, it had risen to nearly 16 ft in 1881 and was 18 ft in 1953. To keep the river out, embankments have had to be raised continuously. In some places along the river you can see timbers bolted on top of the granite embankment walls which were put in place while the Thames Barrier was being built as a temporary defence.

Although the deepening of the river has been recognized for a very long while, it has never been possible to predict with real certainty how high the highest tides will go. It is still not possible—all the calculations are couched in terms of the statistical likelihood of certain conditions occurring. Exceptional tides can be monitored hours ahead, but their level in London can only be calculated within certain margins of error.

The highest Thames tides have been rising steadily over the centuries, and the embankments have had to be raised continuously to keep out flood waters. The river is nearly brimming over here at Cleopatra's Needle in 1932.

If you want to know when high and low water will occur on the river today, you can buy a little book of tables which give estimated times each day. But, as any waterman will confirm, these predictions are only approximate: the tide will turn earlier or later than expected. Those who watch the river day in day out in the control room of the Thames Barrier, now the responsibility of the National Rivers Authority, will tell you that it is not only the timing of high and low water which cannot be accurately gauged: neither can the height of each tide.

The only predictable aspect of the tides is the long-term trend for them to get higher and higher, so that there is an expectation that from the year 2030 the Thames Barrier will be nearing the end of its useful life and some additional kind of flood defence will have to be created. In the meantime, the barrier people have the task of deciding whether or not to go for a 'closure' sealing off the river from the influence of the sea, and closing it to shipping. Since the barrier first began to operate it has been shut in earnest only eight times—four times in 1990. On each occasion the tide turned out not to be hazardous: London would not have drowned had the great, semi-circular, steel gates not been closed.

To understand why the tides are so unpredictable, and why the river is getting deeper over the years, it is best to climb into an imaginary hot-air balloon and float high above the coast of England, with the estuary of the Thames way down below. You will see that the river forms a trumpet at its mouth as it enters the North Sea. Ten thousand years ago, there would have been no east coast: England was joined to the continent. A mass of ice covered all but the southernmost part of the landmass of Britain. A warming of the climate melted the ice which shrank and ran into the sea. Sea levels rose and the Channel was formed, cutting England off from the continent. This thawing has continued, though the rise in sea level has slowed. It is only ice which was on land that raises sea levels as it melts. This is still happening with the glaciers in the mountainous regions of Europe. The Arctic circle is mostly floating ice, and further melting there does not raise sea levels. However, further warming does make the sea expand and raises the level around the coast.

The long and continuous deepening of the Thames has been caused by a rise in sea levels and a tilting of the landmass. Mainland Britain rests on a plate of unstable crust which has been re-balancing itself after the retreat of the ice sheets. As the weight of frozen water has

Cheyne Walk, Chelsea, just before the Victorian embankments were built in 1865. Living by a river is very attractive, and there is a tendency for people to forget about the dangers.

gone, the north-west of Scotland has been rising out of the sea, and the south-east has been sinking into the sea. This is the fundamental cause of the deepening of the tidal reaches of the Thames.

If we look down on this sinking estuary we can see the tides swilling up through the trumpet of the estuary, and swirling inland all the way to Teddington Weir, and over it when the tides are particularly strong and high. The main influence on the strength of the tides is the pull of the sun and the moon which heaves the water around in the North Sea. Every two weeks there are 'spring tides'—the term has nothing to do with the seasons. These high tides occur when the moon and sun pull in the same direction. When they counteract each other there is a 'neap tide'—the difference between low and high water is reduced.

The danger of flooding is obviously greatest when there is a spring tide. If there were no other influences, these tides would be fairly predictable, as would the gradual deepening of the river. But the weather plays a critical part in the flow of tides on the Thames, and it is the weather which poses the great threat to all those who live along the river and to the survival of London.

Chelsea Regatta, in 1865. Although the Victorian embankments have not been built, the riverside is built up against high tides which would otherwise have spread over an extensive area. Embanking the Thames has made it deeper and narrower.

It was the weather that caused the disastrous floods on the east coast in 1953. Freak conditions in the North Sea produced a great surge of water which flooded 160,000 acres of farmland, 24,000 houses, 200 factories, 200 miles of railway, twelve gasworks and two power stations. More than 300 people were drowned—others died of fright and exposure. The toll at Canvey was fifty-eight. Thousands of sheep, cattle, pigs, horses and other livestock perished. London very nearly went under. The cause was a storm in the North Sea.

You often hear on the weather forecast that a 'deep depression' is heading across the Atlantic. This is an area of very low pressure in which the spiralling winds blow hard, as in a whirlpool. If you blow across the surface of a cup of water it banks up on one side, and then falls back when you stop blowing. That is what high winds do to the North Sea. Not only that; the low pressure at the centre of a depression sucks up the water and holds it in a mound.

The tides of the North Sea run down the east coast. If there is a high tide at Aberdeen it can be monitored all the way down to the Thames. In the control room of the Thames Barrier a computer graphic is composed from the tide gauges on the coast showing the tide levels as they are registered on the coast. A low pressure area rounding the north of Scotland will catch hold of the tide and swill it towards the Thames estuary, pushing it way above normal levels.

The actual tide will register way above that predicted. If the weather changes for some reason, and the high north winds abate, then the sea might settle down. But if they persist they will bank up the shallow North Sea and force water into the Thames estuary where it is funnelled inland. It was such weather conditions that caused the 1953 flood, and it is for similar weather conditions that those who operate the Thames Barrier are on the watch. The sophisticated computer models of how the tides will behave cannot cope with the vagaries of North Sea storms: gut feeling as much as the reading of east coast tide gauges is what decides whether or not the barrier should close.

It is not simply the height and strength of a sea surge that is important—the time it lasts is important too. In 1953, London was saved by the fact that the surge abated, and much of it was dissipated as it flowed over the sea walls at Canvey Island, Margate and Southend. The tide was spent by the time it had washed up to London Bridge. Had the sea defences nearer the coast held, then London might have been flooded. And had the surge continued for longer the hollows of the estuary

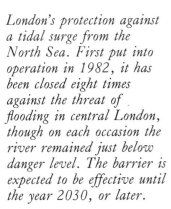

London's protection against a tidal surge from the North Sea. First put into operation in 1982, it has been closed eight times against the threat of flooding in central London, though on each occasion the river remained just below danger level. The barrier is expected to be effective until the year 2030, or later.

would have filled up so that they could take no more and the tide would have pushed further inland.

A general rise in sea levels raises the potential height of exceptional tides, and in that sense increases the risk of flooding in London. But it is not at all clear yet that global warming has made things worse. In the past there have been dips in the upward curve showing a deepening of the river, and it is possible we are in one of those dips now. A statistical analysis of the trends in the highest tides in central London does not show a continuation of the upward drift. But as sea water swashes around, pulled this way and that by the centrifugal force of the sun and the moon, and driven by high winds, a single freak tide is always possible—and it always has been.

There has been a significant rise in sea levels during this century, not because of the melting of the polar ice caps, but because of the expansion of the volume of the sea at higher temperatures and the melting of glaciers. But even without that, flood control would still be a serious issue on the tidal Thames. For centuries, the response to the rising levels of the highest tides was to build higher embankments. While Old London Bridge stood, it effectively blocked the upward tidal flow in London. After it was demolished in the 1830s, the tidal limit became Teddington Weir, though the highest spring tides wash right over it. The embanking of the river, and the dredging of silt to maintain a depth for shipping both have the effect of increasing the velocity of the tides up-river. In its natural state, the river would flood over the low-lying land of the estuary and the force of the tides would be weakened.

A permanent solution to the threat of flooding was first proposed in the nineteenth century when the technology became available to put a permanent barrage across the mouth of the river. Shipping would have had to go through a lock system in the barrage, a considerable inconvenience, and it was understood subsequently that the scheme would have killed off the Port of London within a few years. Upstream of the barrage, the river would have silted up so heavily and quickly that dredging would have become impossible.

When the great Victorian embankments were built by the Metropolitan Board of Works between 1869 and 1874 an estimate was made of the highest possible tides. Owners of riverside properties were asked to comply with the levels set by the Board—17 ft 6 ins. In August 1880 the Board served notices on those who had not raised

The control room at the Thames Barrier that could save London from a disaster greater than the Blitz. Weather conditions in the North Sea, and tide levels right down the east coast are carefully monitored day in, day out.

their riverfront defences to the required level. The following winter on 18 January 1881, the tide reached 17 ft 6 ins at Westminster. *The Times* reported on 19th :

> *Yesterday a calamitous high tide occurred on the Thames, flooding, in addition to many other places, the low-lying neighbourhoods between Blackfriars and Westminster Bridges. The most heartrending scenes were witnessed … The most damage was done to houses lying between Upper Ground Street and Waterloo, many buildings being flooded with 5¹/₂ feet of water … ice floes piled on the Speaker's steps at Westminster.*

Exceptional tides were recorded several times at the end of the nineteenth century, but it was nearly half a century later before a tide similar to that of 1881 occurred. That was in December 1927 when it reached 17 ft 3 ins. Then, in the following year, a new record was set and London experienced its most calamitous flood this century.

On the night of 6–7 January the predicted high water at London Bridge was 12 ft 5 ins to occur at 1.37 a.m. The actual height of the tide, driven by freak winds and swelled by a strong flow of water from up-river, was 18 ft 3 ins. It peaked just after 1 a.m., nearly half an hour earlier than expected. At Millbank a riverside wall collapsed and fourteen people were drowned. At that time there was little in the way of a flood warning system, and anyway, as a government report stated, nobody expected anything like the tide which occurred.

In theory it would have been possible to go on raising the level of embankments all along the river each time there was an exceptional tide, but this eventually became far too costly and impracticable. In the post-war years, when all the riverside wharves below London Bridge and the docks were busy with shipping, a large number of flood defences would have had to be movable—boards put in place when a high tide was expected.

The solution was some kind of barrier. It took a long time to settle on one scheme, and in many ways these were nail-biting years because a tide that would over-top the embankments was always possible. Banks were raised in the early 1970s. Then in 1974 construction of a barrier began at Woolwich. It took eight years to build, and was in operation by October 1982. The gates were closed against a high tide for the first time the following year. Downstream, the riverside defences had to be re-built and raised to hold in the lake of water held by the barrier.

The Victorian embankments being built in 1866. Soon after they were completed they had to be raised because of exceptional tides.

Although the technology that has gone into the construction of the barrier and the continuous monitoring of tides in the control room at Woolwich are impressive, the effects of closing it remain surprisingly experimental. Every month a test on the machinery is carried out, and in the early days the consequences of bringing up the gates at various states of the tide were quite unexpected. Such is the complexity of the movements of water that the point at which the barrier is shut influences the flow of the river, way upstream.

On a couple of occasions the barrier control room received an alarmed phone call from the captain of HMS *Belfast* moored between London Bridge and Tower Bridge. As a result of a closure of the barrier, the flow of the tides had been suddenly halted, producing an abrupt change in the level of the river in London. HMS *Belfast* had shot downstream and tugged at its moorings. A modern mud-lark, out at low water on the shores of the river, experienced a sudden rise in the level which over-topped his boots.

Low tide at Westminster from Joseph Bazalgette's design for the new embankments. Westminster Abbey stands on what was an island before the marshlands of the river flood plain were filled in.

Disconcerting though this was, it demonstrates that the barrier can and will hold the massive weight of Thames water. But in conditions where there might be a tidal surge it is very difficult for those operating the barrier to know when to bring up the gates. If they do so at the fullest and strongest flow of the tides, the backwash can be terrific.

When the barrier was being planned, the Port of London below London Bridge was still working, and the interests of shipping were regarded as important. They still are, even though all the old docks have closed and most of the riverside wharves are abandoned. There are occasions when a flood warning will be issued to people living in Putney, but the barrier will not be closed because the disruption to the ships going into London is judged to be a greater nuisance than the regular and predictable flooding of riverside gardens and embankments upstream. Closing the barrier is also expensive.

Downstream of the barrier there are innumerable flood defences, with gates that come down to hold back the tide, and a 'closure' involves a massive operation. Once the barrier is up, it is assumed that London is safe against tides considerably above those recorded to date. In theory, a flood warning system devised after 1928 with sirens and a procedure for evacuation is still in existence, but since the abolition of the Greater London Council and the building of the barrier, it is difficult to discover exactly how it would work. The official assumption seems to be that it is not needed—yet.

Up-river, beyond Molesey Weir, it is quite a different story. The sea has no influence here, but the weather does. A feature of the river is the broad winter flood meadows which, year in year out, change their character with the seasons. For example, Port Meadow in Oxford floods every winter when the river rises and it is host to flocks of wading birds, redshank, golden plover, lapwings, as well as ducks and geese, which feed on the rich pickings of the saturated ground.

Though the river rises every year with heavy rains, it will generally behave itself for a decade or more, lapping the lawns of riverside gardens, swirling through the locks and rushing white over the weirs. But regularly, much more often than on the tidal Thames, the river spreads out over its flood plain turning into rivers the suburban roads of housing developments in places like Maidenhead. The rise of water is much more predictable here, much more obviously caused by local weather conditions than the North Sea surges which are propelled along the Thames estuary by forces acting hundreds of miles away.

Port Meadow, Oxford, in flood in 1875. Up-river, on the non-tidal reaches of the Thames, flooding has been much more common. Every winter, Port Meadow still floods when rainwater or melting snow swells the river.

Because up-river flooding is caused by different forces, historically it has a calendar of calamity of its own; the most recent disaster year was 1947, not 1953. Whereas down-river the height of tides is inexorably rising in time, up-river the greatest and most devastating floods occurred long ago. They could occur again if similar weather conditions prevailed, and would be devastating because of the increase in the number of people now living in the flood plain of the Thames.

Probably the greatest flood in history on the upper Thames occurred in January 1809. It was a winter of extraordinary weather all over the country, with heavy snowfalls, freezing temperatures and then sudden thaws. The tributaries of the Thames as well as the main river flooded, and there was such a strong flow of fresh water that the weak, neap tides were barely noticeable. The Ravensbourne overflowed and flooded Lewisham and Deptford, damaging the bridges there, but the Wandle did not—such is the unpredictable nature of flooding, for the two rivers have their sources only 100 yards apart. In south London, Kennington and Clapham were flooded.

Freak weather conditions caused the flooding. A layer of frozen rain sealed the ground, and snow fell on this. When the snow melted, it could not be absorbed into the ground because of the ice underneath, and it ran straight into the rivers. The *Gentleman's Magazine* reported that on 28 January:

The Thames over the banks of Boulter's Lock where the road traffic is at the same height as the river.

> *The Exeter mail was near Staines, the coach got into a part where the water was so deep that it floated, and the horses swam. The coach was suddenly thrown over, the coachman and guard thrown to a considerable distance; and the passengers and horses were got out, but the coach could not be. The whole country was covered from Chertsey to Maidenhead; the towns were running with water in torrents as high as the parlour windows. Numbers of the poor have lost their all, which has been carried away in the streams.*

All along the banks of the non-tidal Thames are plaques commemorating the highest water levels reached. These vary from one section of the river to the next, for local conditions influence the height floods reach. At Boulter's Lock, Maidenhead, 1809 was the highest ever flood, followed by 1774, 1795, 1821, 1894 and 1947.

Whereas tidal flooding tends to come in one great fatal rush of water, up-river flooding can persist for days or weeks. The flood of 1947 came in another severe winter of heavy snowfalls and gales, and affected a large part of the Midlands and southern England. In the Thames valley, the water rose alarmingly on 11 March when a thaw melted snow in the Cotswolds, the Windsor-Maidenhead road was cut off and Maidenhead and Marlow were flooded to quite a depth by 13 March. Tens of thousands of homes were marooned and people rescued from the upper floors of their houses. There were more blizzards on 15 March, and the water at Teddington continued to rise until 20th.

George Kenyon lived on an island in the River Thames near Weybridge in 1947:

When the flood was rising we were still going backwards and forwards to work, which we did in the dinghy every day. It was tied up to the veranda of our bungalow in the end—we were going straight off from there. At times furniture came sweeping down the river, so on one or two occasions we tried to do a bit of salvage work and I went out in the dinghy one day and lassoed a wardrobe. I was trying to bring this thing ashore, rather like a cowboy with a mad cow, but in the end we were drifting down into the main weir at Weybridge which was absolutely foaming at the time. So I had to cast it off and let it go, which was a bit of a snag, because furniture was very hard to come by at that time. When the water actually came through the floor we decided to leave. In one bungalow there was a lovely baby grand piano with the water lashing the keyboards and some refugee wildfowl sitting on the top of the piano.

There is no reason why a flood on the scale of 1947 could not happen again. Although the National Rivers Authority has the responsibility to deal with the problem, and there are now proposals to cut a channel to carry flood waters away from vulnerable areas, there is nothing ultimately that can be done to prevent another major flood. In fact, those who seek to discern a pattern in the historical records suggest the upper Thames valley is due for another inundation of the 1947 level soon. It was a one in fifty-six years event. There have been many lesser floods since 1947 which have caused a great deal of hardship even if they have not been classed as real calamities.

An intriguing piece of work by the Flood Hazard Research Centre of Middlesex Polytechnic has attempted to discover what people living by the Thames believe the threat of flooding to be, and whether or not they imagine anything can be done about it. The degree of optimism is quite remarkable. One of the reasons for this appears to be that the movement of population in the Thames valley is such that few people have in their own lifetimes experienced a really serious flood. Only twelve per cent of those interviewed in the Research Centre's survey remembered the 1947 flood, and only a small proportion of those people still lived in the same place as in 1947.

Although a quarter of the sample of nearly 500 people had some experience of flooding, they seemed to believe that the benefits of living by the river, because it was pleasant and convenient for work, outweighed the disadvantages. There was evidently a great deal of wishful thinking and fatalism in attitudes to the hazards of living by the Thames.

Classic London Transport posters of the Twenties: the dreamy image of the Thames at Staines and Kingston.

There is absolutely no doubt that the Thames will continue over-flowing its banks upstream of Teddington from time to time. Below there on the tidal river flood defences will almost certainly have to be raised in future to avoid a catastrophe. Most of those whose job it is to study tides and sea levels and flood defences believe that we have about forty or fifty years to decide what to do next. And, whatever the hardships flooding may cause down on the estuary or upstream, they are an utterly different problem from that of a major flood in the centre of London's great metropolis.

This was the conclusion of the definitive study of the problem in 1968 by Professor Hermann Bondi, an astronomer, who was asked by the then Ministry of Housing and Local Government to examine the proposal for the barrier. At the time, a powerful voice in the plans for flood prevention was the Port of London Authority which was very much concerned with the interests of shipping. Even in 1968, Professor Bondi believed the river above Tilbury would carry a considerable amount of shipping, and many of the problems relative to the siting and design of the barrier were to do with keeping the navigational channels clear.

Within twelve years of the Bondi report, all the docks above the Woolwich barrier had closed down and very few commercial ships of any size now come through the shining steel helmets of the barrier's piers. Professor Bondi had preferred a permanent barrier, with a locking system to allow boats through, but considered it impractical at the time. He believed it would improve the 'look' of the river in the centre of town for it would no longer be tidal, and he thought the banks unsightly at low tide. At high tide the Thames was 'one of the great sights of the world, to be put well above Paris and in the same class as Leningrad'.

CONTEMPLATING THE FUTURE

The astronomical cost of protecting central London from the possibility of an exceptionally high tide is easily justified by contemplation of the cost of such a disaster. A permanent barrier will doubtless be a proposal considered again in the future, if the sea continues to rise in relation to the land. Downstream of the barrier it is not so certain that the costs of keeping out the sea will be considered worth the saving of places like Canvey Island, which already cowers beneath high defensive walls.

Since the founding of Londinium by the Romans, the great power of the Thames has been a force for both good and evil, and it will continue to be so. The scale of modern technology is such that it can contain the ocean tides—when divers were working to recover the bodies from the wreckage of the *Marchioness* in August 1989, the Woolwich barrier was closed to hold back the flood tide and to make the work less difficult. This successful Canute-like demonstration of the barrier's effectiveness against normal tides has not convinced everybody that it is any use. The fact is that nobody knows for certain how high the next record tide will be.

Yet tens of thousands of commuters still cross the river each morning on their way to work in central London, many of them going to offices which are well below the high-water mark. In this respect, Londoners are no different from the millions who live in Holland below sea level or the people of San Francisco who live and work in a city which is liable to be ripped apart by an earthquake.

The very worst possible flood conditions have never been experienced on the Thames. This would be a North Sea surge, which coincided exactly with the highest point of a spring tide, and a flood of fresh water from above the tidal limits of the river. It might be that in breaching defences at the estuary, and spreading out over its flood plain above London, the force of the river might be weakened. Or it might be that a statistically highly unlikely event actually occurs, and the water is funnelled into London over the barrier. In 1962, a surge tide went fourteen feet above the predicted level in Hamburg, Germany, and 20,000 people had to be evacuated. Nobody can say with certainty that London could not be flooded.

All that can be said is that it is extremely unlikely that the Thames will spill over the embankments in the centre of London. Meanwhile, the saddest aspect of the Thames is how little it is used, in a City choked with road traffic, and that the miles of timber wharves, which have withstood so many tides, and held fast so many ships, are left abandoned and rotting. Some day the river will be taken seriously again, not simply because from time to time it threatens to rise and engulf the great metropolis to which it gave rise, but because it has found a new value for Londoners. Now that it is clean again and wildlife is returning it could become more and more a place for pleasure, a valued part of London's landscape, a natural force still flowing through the heart of one of the world's great cities.

The new face of London's riverside: the refurbished Billingsgate fish market, designed by the Richard Rogers Partnership.

INDEX

ACKNOWLEDGEMENTS

Author's acknowledgements

For all the hundreds of books about the Thames, there are very few people who have a profound knowledge of more than a fraction of its fascinating history, from the source to the estuary. I am deeply indebted to those who have given me their time and their wisdom on a very wide range of subjects. Chris Ellmers, Keeper of the Museum in Docklands at the Museum of London, Robin Craig and Sarah Palmer gave invaluable help on the story of shipping and the Port of London. On London's early history, Gustav Milne, John Clark, Jim Sewell and all those at the Museum of London and the City of London Corporation were very helpful. John Graham-Leigh of Thames Water was a mine of information on the history of drinking water, as were those at Kew Steam Museum. Alwyne Wheeler provided the history of Thames fisheries, and Steve Colclough of the National Rivers Authority brought the story up to date. Richard Burnell steered me in the right direction on rowing. On flooding, a special thanks to John Gardiner and to John Hounslow and the team at the Thames Barrier. A great many other people, far too numerous to mention, provided invaluable detail. I would also like to thank all those who provided their memories of the Thames, only a few of which could be included in the book. Sarah, Mark and Michelle in the London Weekend Television library were a wonderful support as always, unearthing many obscure books with great efficiency and speed. Deryn Cox provided dedication and interest to the task of keeping the Thames book and series going, while Stephanie Tillotson and Louise Brodie spent long hours finding and interviewing those with memories of the Thames. A special thanks to Louise and the Museum of London for delving into the files of their living memory project. Finally, thanks to Philippa Lewis for painstaking picture research, and to Gabrielle Townsend and Jennifer Chilvers at Collins & Brown for organizing the publication of the book in record time.

Acknowledgements of illustrations

Aerofilms 152; Bridgeman Art Library cover illustration 7 27 (Guildhall), 35 (Guildhall), 42 47 (Guildhall), 51 (Guildhall), 63 (Guildhall), 70–1 (Guildhall), 82–3 (Guildhall), 85 86–7 (Guildhall), 91 (Museum of London), 95 114–115 118–9 (Guildhall), 122–3 131 (Guildhall), 146–7 151 (Guildhall); British Library 20; British Museum 24 102–3 126 127 147; Trustees of the Chatsworth Collection 67; Christie's Colour Library 2 20 27 98 138–9; Corporation of London Records Office 64 130; Fitzwilliam Museum, Cambridge 6; Francis Frith Collection 9 96 97; Guildhall 41 69 106 132 133; Hulton Picture Company 112–13 141 145 150 153; Imperial War Museum 58–9; Philippa Lewis 25 89 116; London Docklands Development Corporation 61 94; London Transport Museum 155; Mansell Collection 18 21 38 40 64–5 80–1 83 84 85 88 104 105 124–5 128 129 136 137; Mary Evans Picture Library 101; Museum in Docklands Project 24–5 36 37 48 49 54 55 56 57 59 72 73 78 79 108 109 137; Museum of London 11 14 16 17 23 74–5 76 94 103 116 117 121 123; National Maritime Museum 1 3 12 13 19 22 26 28 29 32 33 44 45 52 53 77 90 92 93 108–9 110–11 136; Oxford Central Library 100 109 152; Private Collection 30–1; Richard Rogers Partnership 157; Marquess of Salisbury 142–3; Tate Gallery 107 135; Thames Water Authority 148 149; TUC Archive 39, Captain R. Williamson 12; Cy Young 93 111.